HELLO!

CALLING ALL FOOTBALL FANS!

WELCOME TO YOUR COMPLETE GUIDE TO THE WORLD OF FOOTBALL! WE'RE CELEBRATING THE GREATEST PLAYERS IN THE GAME, THE MOST ICONIC TEAMS, EPIC RIVALRIES, CUP WINNERS AND SO MUCH MORE! IF YOU'RE TRYING FOR A HAT-TRICK IN EA SPORTS FC 25, OR LOOKING TO BUILD YOUR ULTIMATE DREAM TEAM, WE'VE GOT YOU COVERED! FROM JUDE BELLINGHAM TO MESSI TO BONMATI, WE'VE GOT ALL THE STARS YOU LOVE INSIDE, AND THE GAMES YOU JUST CAN'T GET ENOUGH OF. BACK O' THE NET!

Pics: © 2025 Electronic Arts Inc., Shutterstock (4)

THE TEAM

CONTENT EDITOR:
Sarah-Jane Crawford

CONTENT PRODUCERS:
Rebekah McVey
Cara Scott-Morrison
Leah Barton

PRODUCTION MANAGER:
Cheryl Gilbert

DESIGN LEAD:
Craig McGregor

EDITORIAL DIRECTOR:
Gareth Whelan

DESIGNERS:
Jon Fairrie
Emma Power

CONTRIBUTOR:
Alan Watson

Published in the UK by DC Thomson & Co Ltd © DC Thomson & Co Ltd (2025). Registered Office: DC Thomson & Co Ltd, Courier Buildings, 2 Albert Square, Dundee, Scotland, DD1 9QJ. Whilst every reasonable care will be taken neither DC Thomson & Co Ltd, nor its agents accept liability for loss or damage to colour transparencies or any other material submitted to this publication. Distributed by Frontline Ltd, Stuart House, St John's St, Peterborough, Cambridgeshire, PE1 5DD. Tel: +44 (0) 1733 555161 www.frontlinedistribution.co.uk. EU Representative Office: DC Thomson & Co Ltd c/o Findmypast Ireland, RBK House, Irishtown, Athlone, Co. Westmeath. N37 XP52. REPUBLIC OF IRELAND

DC THOMSON

EXPORT DISTRIBUTION (excluding AU and NZ) by: Seymour Distribution Ltd, 2 East Poultry Avenue, London EC1A 9PT. Tel: +44 (0) 20 7429 4000 www.seymour.co.uk.

Enquiries: ultimateseries@dcthomson.co.uk

WHAT'S INSIDE?

TALKING TACTICS!

Before you take to the pitch with your team, here are some tips worth remembering to help you dominate the game in EA SPORTS FC 25!

DODGE DEFENCE

Use Skill Moves at the right time to create goal-scoring opportunities! Fake Shot is a basic but effective move that will send defenders in the wrong direction.

TACTICAL FOULING

Professional fouls can stop attacks, but doing it too often will result in a yellow or red card. Be strategic with it and remember to use a player who hasn't already been booked!

THROWING SMART

To keep possession safe, use short, accurate throws. If you spot a chance, a long throw can reach players further up the pitch, shifting the attack and catching the defence off guard while keeping control of the ball!

CORNER KICKS

■ In a corner kick setup, aim for the back post or the penalty spot where taller players can out-jump defenders for a powerful header!

GOAL GETTER

■ From Trivela to Finesse, there are several ways to get the ball in the back of the net. If you're ever unsure, a regular shot is always a solid choice!

TOP TIP

Always make sure your target is in a good position to receive the ball!

SPREAD OUT

■ Keep your players spread out and covering the entire pitch. This creates more passing options which is crucial when the opposing team pressures you!

ULTIMATE TEAM

TIPS!

■ Ultimate Team is the most popular mode in **FC 25** and gamers from around the world compete in Division Rivals and Champions. If you want to succeed in Ultimate Team, then follow these tips to maximise your chances!

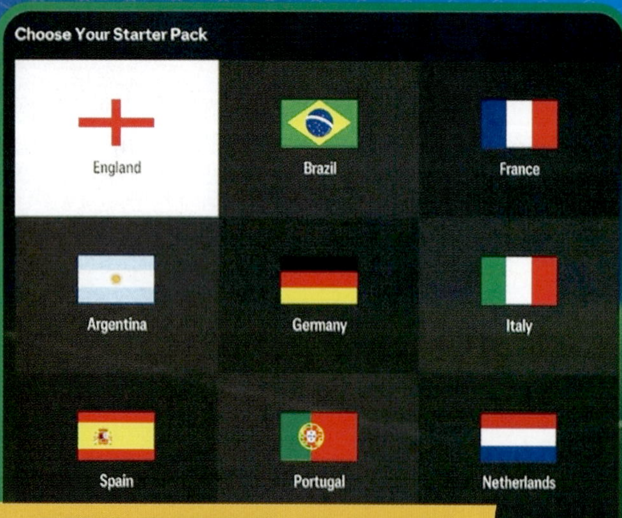

STARTER PACK

■ When you first begin Ultimate Team, you'll select a starter pack – based on one nation. You can select from nine big nations in the game, including England, France, Spain and Brazil. Choosing from the likes of Spain or France is sometimes a better option than England given they have more cheap players available to snap up.

LOAN PLAYER

■ At the outset you can also choose a talented loan player to join your team for a few matches. Decide what position you want to have a top player in the most and then choose a loan player who plays there.

OBJECTIVES

■ Whether it's seven sets of simple initial challenges such as 'buy one player' or 'play a Rivals match' or more complex Squad Building Challenges, these are an important part of FC 25 Ultimate Team. If you regularly complete them, you can earn XP, packs and coins.

VALUE

■ The value of players can go up and down. It's important to keep an eye on the market and try to take advantage of price fluctuations. You might choose to sell a player while his value is high to reinvest in other players. Some good players may also be selling cheap for a time, making it a good time to buy!

BRONZE

■ Buying cheap bronze packs to start off with and then selling a few players from each pack can be another way to build up a profit.

OFFLINE MODE

■ At the start of the game your team will be lacking in quality across the pitch, it's therefore best to start in the Squad Battles offline mode. Here you can choose any difficulty from beginner to Ultimate, giving you the chance to build confidence and earn more points.

EVOLUTIONS

■ Evolutions allows you to upgrade lower-rated cards via challenges, which could lead to some of your players becoming super-powered. Look out for free cards early on.

CHEMISTRY

■ Once you've earned some virtual coins by completing tasks and winning matches, you'll want to get on with building a top team. In FC 25, you can get a team chemistry of 33. A player's chemistry depends on his team-mates. If one player has a link to another via their nationality, league they play in or club they play for, then the chemistry they have together will be higher.

PATIENCE

■ Building a top team takes time. You'll need to build up virtual coins and get lucky with any packs you open. With coins in the bank, it's tempting to rush into buying players right away. However, you might buy players for positions you're already strong in or that aren't any better than what you already have, so always think it through!

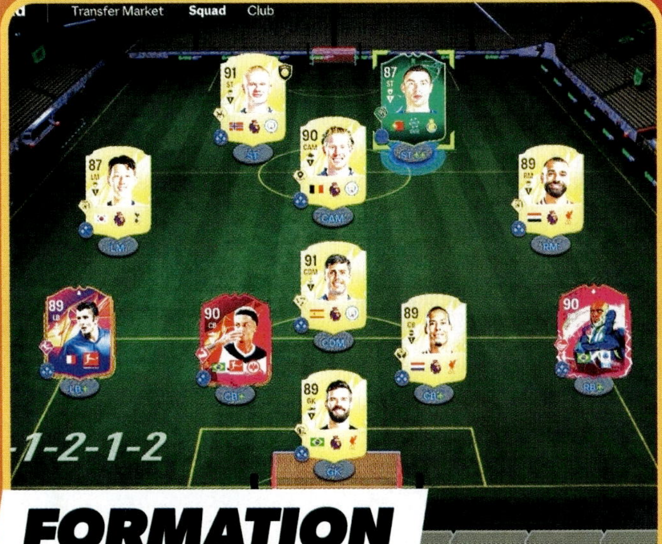

FORMATION

■ It's important to choose a formation that suits your playing style. You'll be playing in lots of matches, and you'll enjoy it more if you can master a style that works for you. It's important also that you have players that fit the formation.

PLAYERS!

■ **Want to know the top 20 highest rated players in EA SPORTS FC 25? Then look no further...**

1 KYLIAN MBAPPÉ

(ST, REAL MADRID) – 91

■ **Mbappé** may have had a tricky start to life at Real Madrid, but he remains one of the world's greatest players and is more than worthy of his 91 rating!

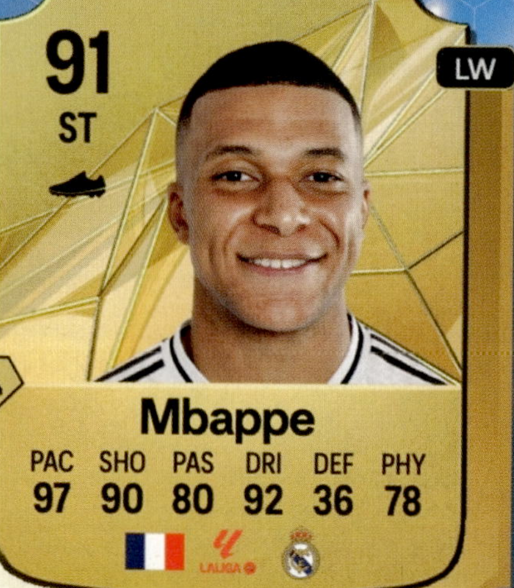

2 RODRI

(CDM, MANCHESTER CITY) – 91

■ In October 2024, **Rodri** became the first Manchester City player to win the Ballon d'Or, cementing his place at the best defensive midfielder on the planet.

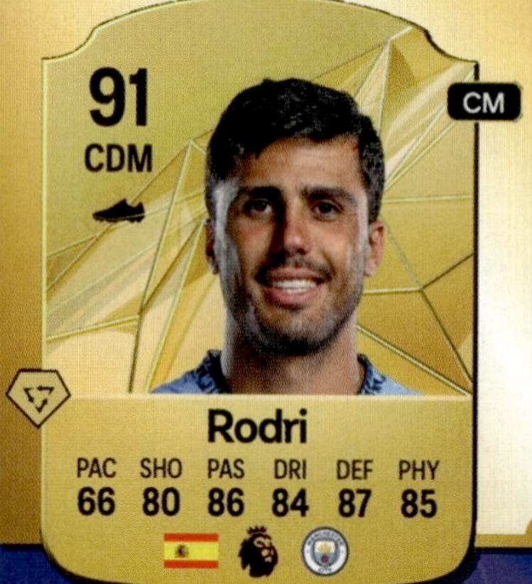

3 AITANA BONMATI

(CM, BARCELONA) – 91

■ Like **Rodri**, **Aitana** won the Ballon d'Or, making her the greatest women's footballer in the world.

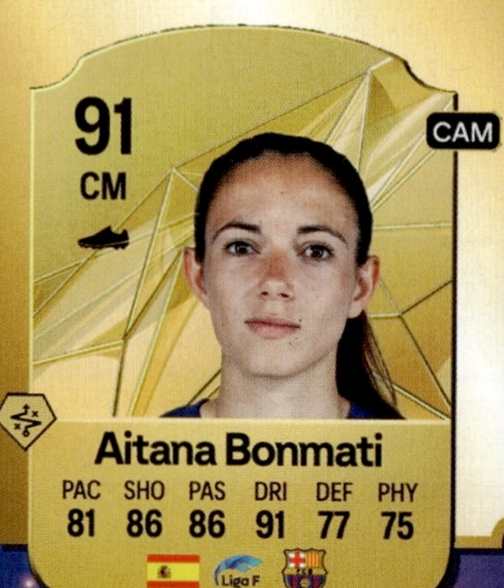

4 ERLING HAALAND

(ST, MANCHESTER CITY) – 91

■ After a second successive Premier League Golden Boot season in 2023/24, **Haaland** may feel he should be **FC 25** top dog. Either way, he's not far off top spot and an asset to any team!

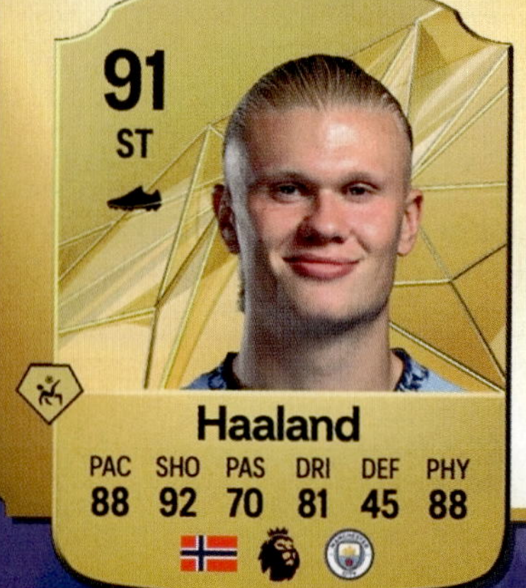

05

90
CAM · CM

Bellingham

PAC	SHO	PAS	DRI	DEF	PHY
80	87	83	88	78	83

JUDE BELLINGHAM
(CAM, REAL MADRID) – 90

09

90
CM · CAM

De Bruyne

PAC	SHO	PAS	DRI	DEF	PHY
67	87	94	87	65	78

KEVIN DE BRUYNE
(CM, MANCHESTER CITY) – 90

13

89
GK

Donnarumma

DIV	HAN	KIC	REF	SPD	POS
90	84	73	90	52	87

GIANLUIGI DONNARUMMA
(GK, PARIS SG) – 89

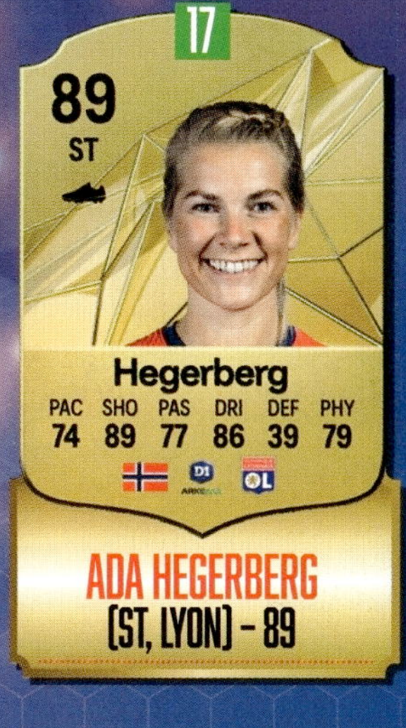

17

89
ST

Hegerberg

PAC	SHO	PAS	DRI	DEF	PHY
74	89	77	86	39	79

ADA HEGERBERG
(ST, LYON) – 89

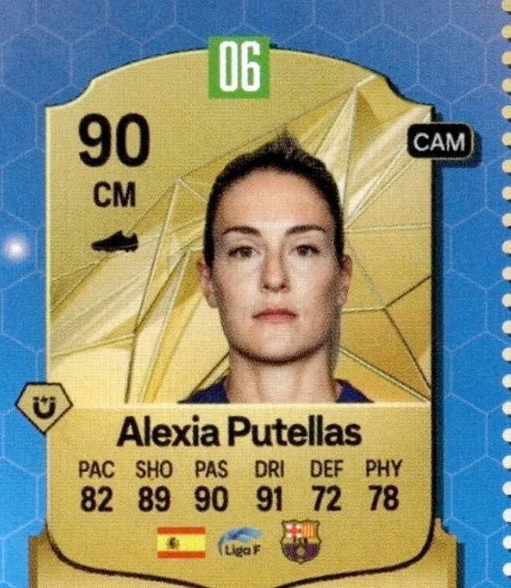

06

90
CM · CAM

Alexia Putellas

PAC	SHO	PAS	DRI	DEF	PHY
82	89	90	91	72	78

ALEXIA PUTELLAS
(CM, BARCELONA) – 90

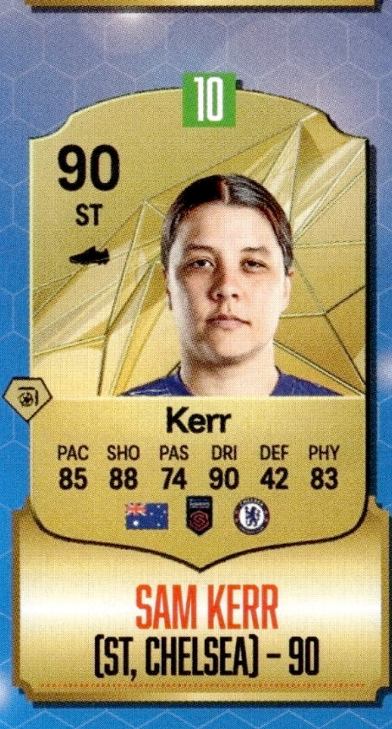

10

90
ST

Kerr

PAC	SHO	PAS	DRI	DEF	PHY
85	88	74	90	42	83

SAM KERR
(ST, CHELSEA) – 90

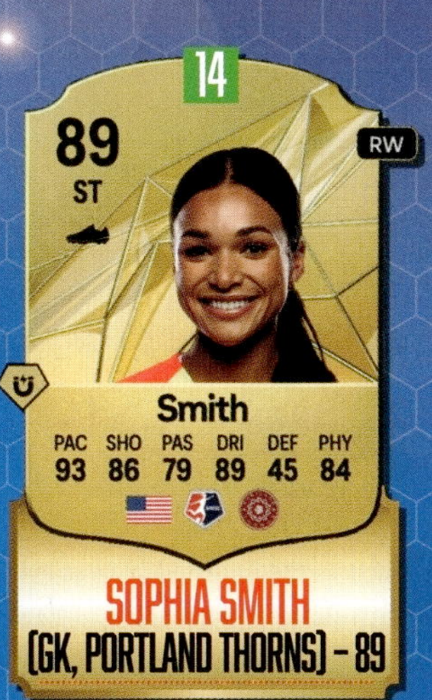

14

89
ST · RW

Smith

PAC	SHO	PAS	DRI	DEF	PHY
93	86	79	89	45	84

SOPHIA SMITH
(GK, PORTLAND THORNS) – 89

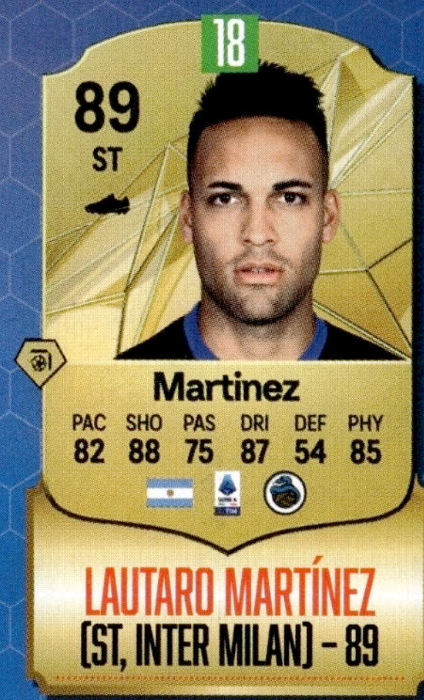

18

89
ST

Martinez

PAC	SHO	PAS	DRI	DEF	PHY
82	88	75	87	54	85

LAUTARO MARTÍNEZ
(ST, INTER MILAN) – 89

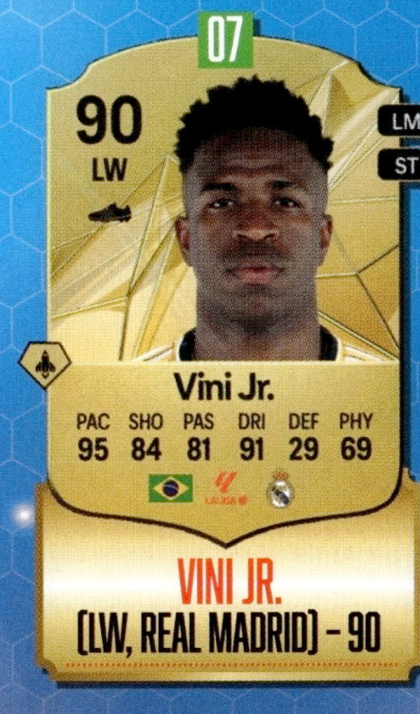

07

90
LW · LM · ST

Vini Jr.

PAC	SHO	PAS	DRI	DEF	PHY
95	84	81	91	29	69

VINI JR.
(LW, REAL MADRID) – 90

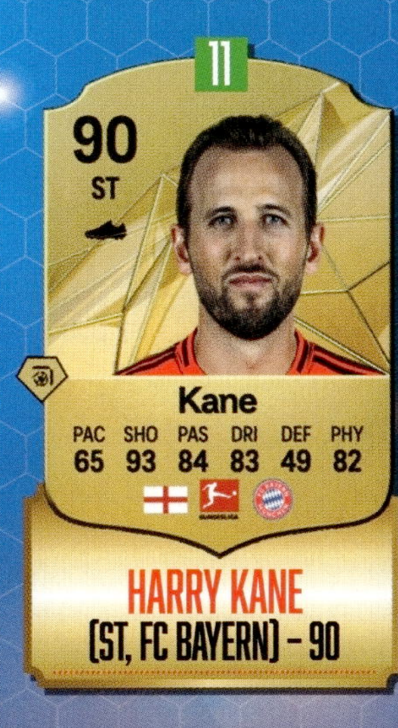

11

90
ST

Kane

PAC	SHO	PAS	DRI	DEF	PHY
65	93	84	83	49	82

HARRY KANE
(ST, FC BAYERN) – 90

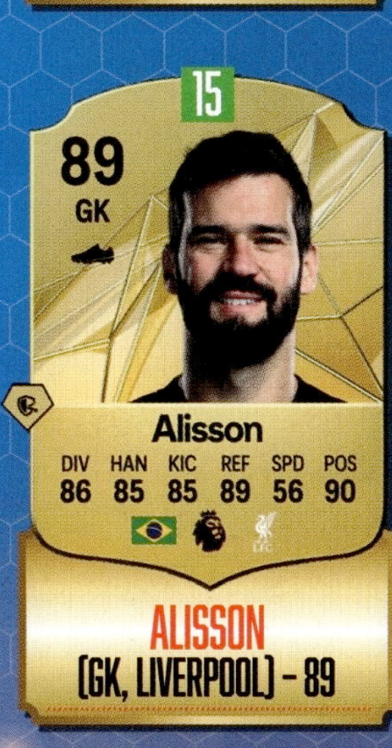

15

89
GK

Alisson

DIV	HAN	KIC	REF	SPD	POS
86	85	85	89	56	90

ALISSON
(GK, LIVERPOOL) – 89

19

89
CB

Mapi Leon

PAC	SHO	PAS	DRI	DEF	PHY
75	73	83	76	90	82

MAPI LEÓN
(CB, BARCELONA) – 89

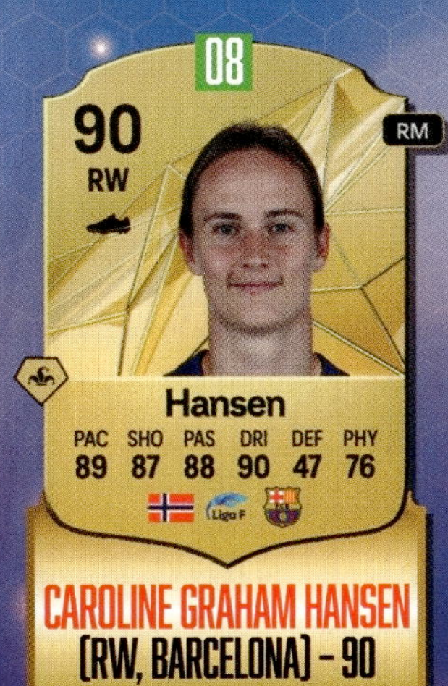

08

90
RW · RM

Hansen

PAC	SHO	PAS	DRI	DEF	PHY
89	87	88	90	47	76

CAROLINE GRAHAM HANSEN
(RW, BARCELONA) – 90

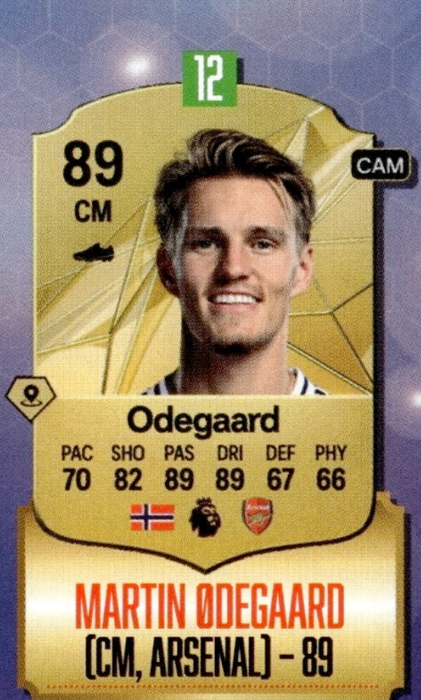

12

89
CM · CAM

Odegaard

PAC	SHO	PAS	DRI	DEF	PHY
70	82	89	89	67	66

MARTIN ØDEGAARD
(CM, ARSENAL) – 89

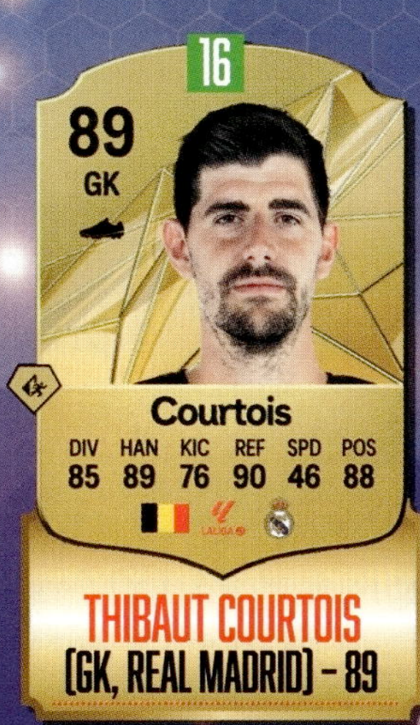

16

89
GK

Courtois

DIV	HAN	KIC	REF	SPD	POS
85	89	76	90	46	88

THIBAUT COURTOIS
(GK, REAL MADRID) – 89

20

89
CB

van Dijk

PAC	SHO	PAS	DRI	DEF	PHY
78	60	71	71	89	86

VIRGJL VAN DIJK
(CB, LIVERPOOL) – 89

Shutterstock (1)

SKILL SCHOOL

■ **OTHER NOTABLE 3 STAR SKILLS:**

Heel Flick – Flick right stick forward and back, roulette right/left
– spin right stick 360 degrees right/left from forward.
Stutter Feint – Hold L2/LB + right stick left then right or right stick right then left.

4 STAR SKILL

Heel To Heel

WHAT IS IT?

Use the front foot heel when running to flick the ball back and then use the back foot heel to flick the ball forward again for a speed boost away from defender.

HOW DO I DO IT?

Flick right stick forward then back.

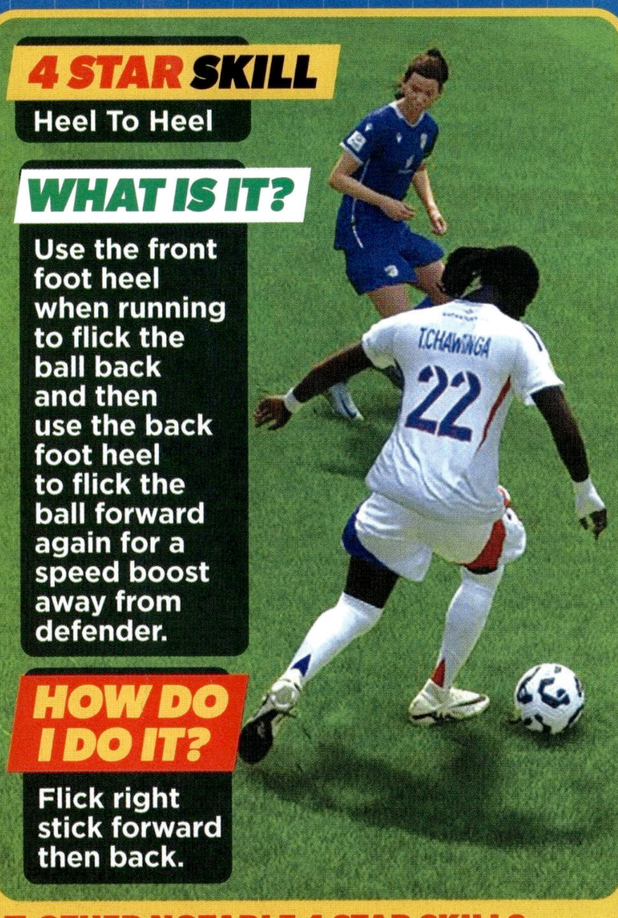

■ **OTHER NOTABLE 4 STAR SKILLS:**
Ball Roll Drag – Hold L1/LB + flick right stick forward then left or right.

5 STAR SKILL

Neymar Rainbow Flick

WHAT IS IT?

Neymar flicks the ball from behind him over his head to the front.

HOW DO I DO IT?

Flick Right stick Left and then Right

■ **OTHER NOTABLE 5 STAR SKILLS:**
Elastico – Spin right stick 180 degrees from right to left behind player.

1 STAR SKILL

First Time Feint Turn

WHAT IS IT?

When approaching the defender roll the ball and drop your shoulder in a different direction to pull away from the defender.

HOW DO I DO IT?

Hold L1/LB + R1/RB + flick left stick back.

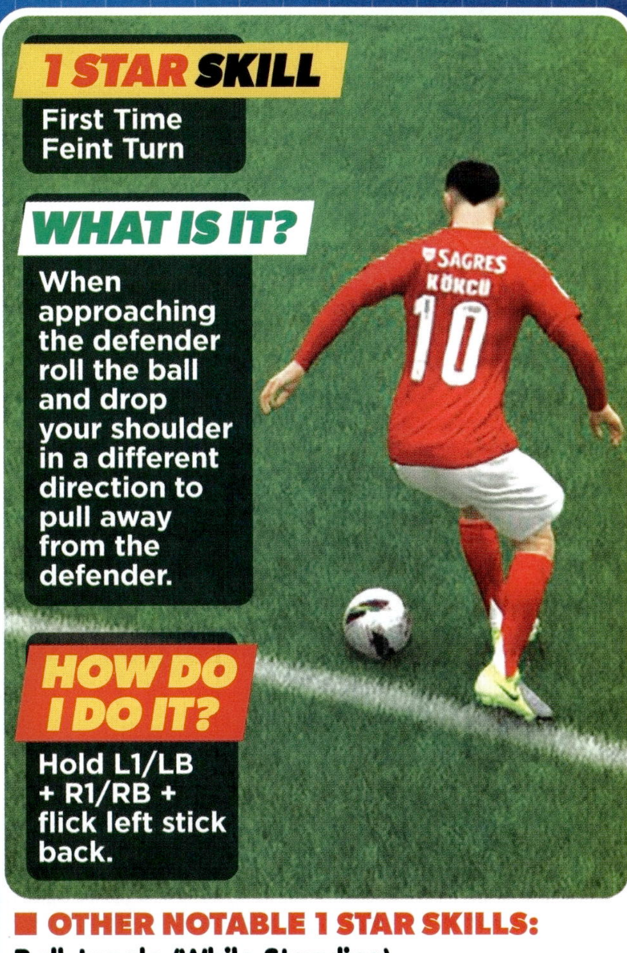

■ **OTHER NOTABLE 1 STAR SKILLS:**
Ball Juggle (While Standing) – L2/LT + Tap R1/RB.

2 STAR SKILL

Drag Back

WHAT IS IT?

Approach your opponent and when he attempts to tackle, drag back and change direction.

HOW DO I DO IT?

L1/LB + R1/RB + Flick left stick back.

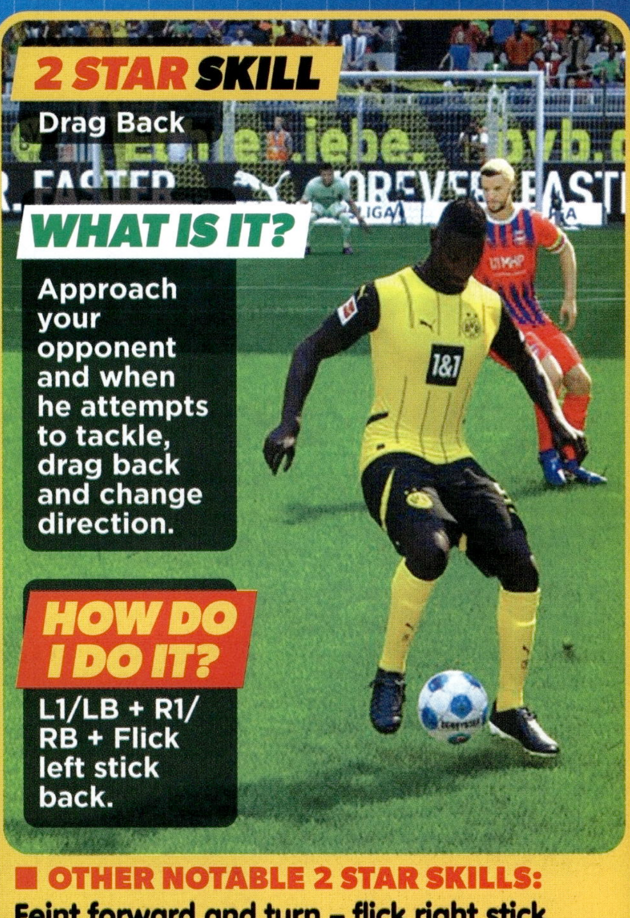

■ **OTHER NOTABLE 2 STAR SKILLS:**
Feint forward and turn – flick right stick back twice.

EA SPORTS FC25
FOOTBALL QUIZ!
IS EAS FC 25 THE FOOTBALL GAME FOR YOU?
START HERE
Scoring a goal is the best feeling ever.
YES
NO
Playing is always better than watching.
You watch YouTubers do gaming Let's Plays.
You know everything about your fave team.
NO
NO
YES
YES
Ultimate Team is your favourite part of EAS FC 25.
NO
YES
VLAHOVIC
9
You prefer football to cars.
NO
NO
YES
You dream of being a football star.
NO
You have a favourite football player.
YES
NO
You love to level up and tweak your stats in games.
YES
YES
NO
YES
EA SPORTS FC25
For you, it doesn't get better than EAS FC 25! This video game has all the top players and the most realistic gameplay ever!
ROCKET LEAGUE
Football is great, but rocket cars make it even better. You care much more about having fun than being realistic!
FOOTBALL MANAGER
You'd rather run the top teams than play for them and that's awesome. No-one knows more about football than you!

1 SPOT THE BALL!

Circle the original ball in this shot! Can you spot the real from the fakes?

2 NAME THAT TEAM BADGE!

- T_T_EN_A_ H_T_P_R
- I_T_R M_L_N
- W__V_S
- A_L_T_CO MA_R__
- W__T H__

3 MEGA MATCH!

Match the player to their team!

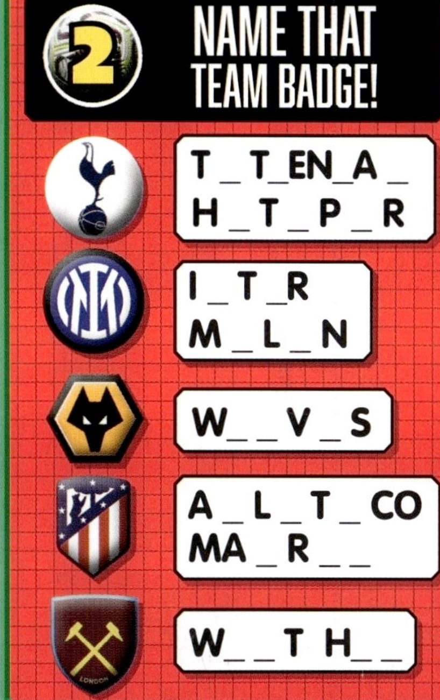

SPEED!

■ Pace can really destroy teams and having some of the quickest players in **FC 25** can give you a greater chance of success! Check out this list of top 10 speed merchants to keep an eye on...

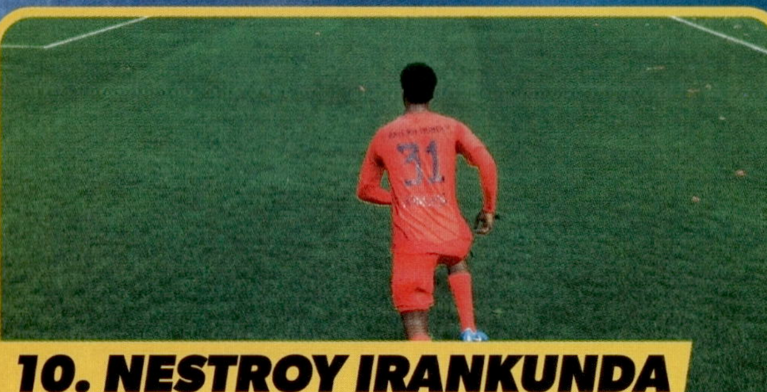

10. NESTROY IRANKUNDA (94) | RM

■ With pace to burn, Bayern Munich's young Australian midfielder is one to watch. Not quite a first team regular yet, but he'll improve over time and add to stats which are already decent.

9. RAFAEL LEÃO (94) | LW

■ The AC Milan winger is a dream pick up in **FC 25** with excellent stats across pace, dribbling and passing. His shooting stats are also pretty good, meaning he can score and assist.

8. TABITHA CHAWINGA (94) | RM

■ Lyon striker Chawinga has pace which makes her second only in striker terms behind Mbappé. With good dribbling skills of 84, she's also strong playing out wide.

7. YANKUBA MINTEH (95) | RM

■ The Gambian midfielder isn't strong across the stats board but does excel on the pace front with a 95 stat. Playing in the Premier League also makes him a solid choice for increasing the chemistry level in Ultimate Team.

6. THEO HERNÁNDEZ (95) | LB

■ AC Milan's France international left-back is an elite level option in **FC 25**. With pace stats of 95 and high numbers across dribbling, defending and physical metrics, **Hernández** offers high-level stats across every field.

5. MOUSSA DIABY (95) | RM

■ Now playing for Al-Ittihad in the Saudi Pro League, **Diaby** is a solid right-sided option with 95 pace and 86 dribbling stats.

4. ALPHONSO DAVIES (95) | LB

■ A lack of top Canadian players in major European leagues means that **Davies'** nationality doesn't help much with improving chemistry in Ultimate Team. However, with 95 pace and 84 dribbling stats, he remains a great option.

3. VINI JR. (95) | LW

■ After **Mbappé**, **Vini Jr.** is the most skilful player at Real Madrid and undoubted the best winger in the game. His dribbling skills are unmatched to the level he'll give defenders nightmares!

2. KARIM ADEYEMI (96) | LM

■ **Adeyemi** doesn't have the greatest physical stat – only 70 – with his shooting not much better at 73. However, with searing 96 pace, he makes for a great option on the counterattack.

1. KYLIAN MBAPPÉ (97) | ST

■ The best player in the game also happens to be the fastest. With high shooting and dribbling skills also sitting at 90+, he is super hard to defend against.

EA SPORTS FC25

8 GR8 WAYS TO SCORE EVERY TIME!

Do you want some absolute tekkers tips to make sure you are hitting the back of the net more often? Then get reading before scoring!

CHIP SHOT

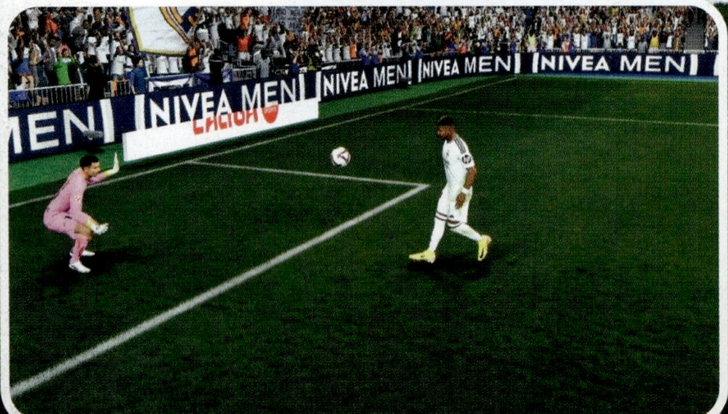

This finish is a delicate kick that lifts the ball over a defender or goalkeeper. Try it out by running towards the goalie and when they come out of the box, press L1/LB + Shoot.

INSIDE BOX ACROSS THE KEEPER

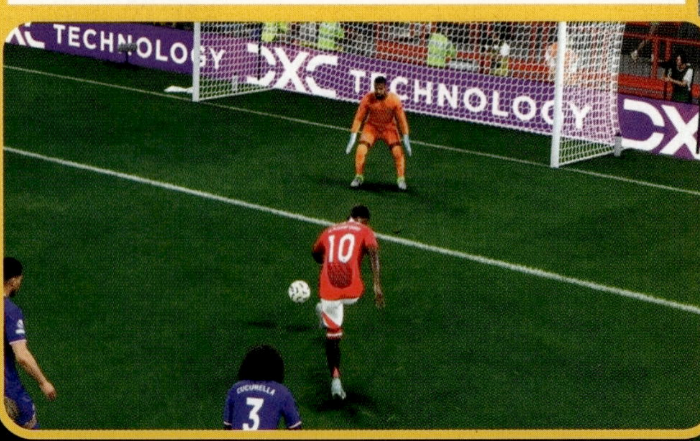

A nice way to confuse the goalkeeper into not knowing which corner you're going for. Try by approaching a penalty spot at an angle, aim across the goalie and shoot.

HEADER FROM CORNER

■ It helps if you have someone on your team who has strong header stats. If you do, aim for them in the middle, 75% power on a cross and then shoot.

CUT BACK

■ Lots of players love scoring this way and it can be hard to defend against. When arriving in the box, go towards the byline and, as the goalkeeper or defender comes across towards your player, pass back across box to a free player and shoot.

FREE KICK

■ Scoring free kicks can be difficult but not impossible. Look to aim between the wall and the goalkeeper, 90% power and shoot, left foot player on left and right foot player on right.

FINESSE SHOT

■ The finesse shot is one taken with the inside of the boot and good for using to find the far corner of the goal. Approach the goalkeeper at an angle from right or left and when close press R1/RB + shoot.

POWER SHOT

■ The power shot has been given an upgrade in **EAS FC 25** and is now more powerful than ever! When you're just inside box (or outside the box) aim at goal and press L1+R1/LB+RB + shoot.

LONG RANGE FINESSE SHOT

■ If taking a finesse shot from outside the box, always consider the player's strongest foot. When outside the box, approach at an angle and Curl Shot with ¾ power pressing R1/RB + shoot.

In **EA SPORTS FC 25** Career Mode, signing players who are already among the very best in the world isn't achievable for most. However, signing a talented wonderkid as early as possible before their price tag becomes sky high is a strategy worth pursuing. Check out some of the most talented goalkeepers aged 21 and under that you should be looking out for!

GOALKEEPER WONDERKIDS

PLAYER: GUILLAUME RESTES
CLUB: TOULOUSE
CURRENT RATING: 78
POTENTIAL RATING: 88

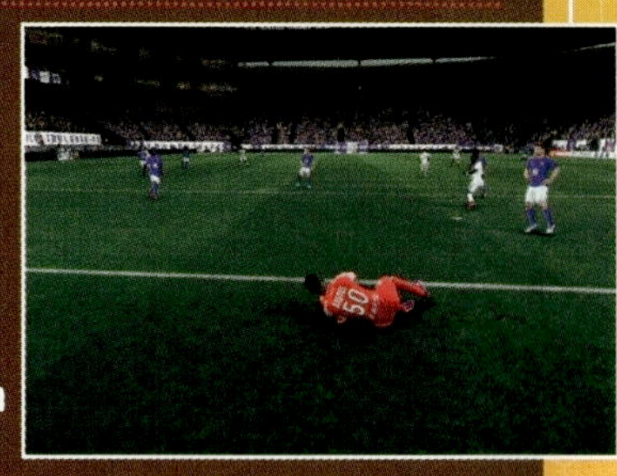

Born in 2005, this young goalkeeper has already made over 50 appearances for the Toulouse first-team in Ligue 1. With super-quick reflexes and excellent positional awareness, he has the potential to be the main man for France in the years to come.

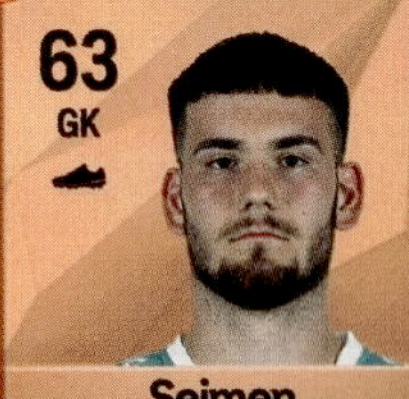

PLAYER: DENNIS SEIMEN
CLUB: STUTTGART
CURRENT RATING: 63
POTENTIAL RATING: 84

In 2024 Stuttgart extended Seimen's contract until June 2029, fully aware they have a very promising goalkeeper on their books. While his current rating isn't high, he has lots of room to grow and could one day be in your first-team with the right development training.

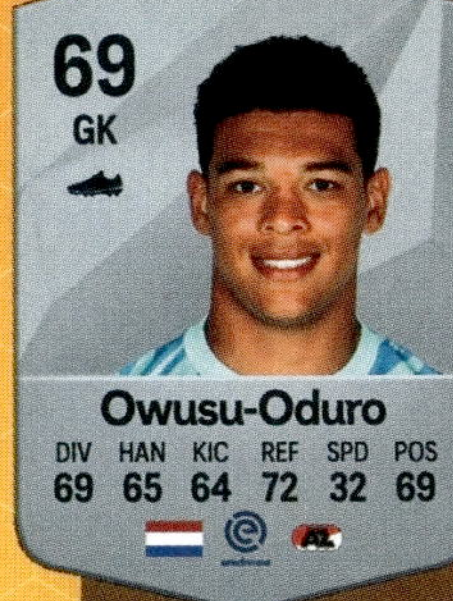

69 GK

Owusu-Oduro

DIV	HAN	KIC	REF	SPD	POS
69	65	64	72	32	69

PLAYER: ROME-JAYDEN OWUSU-ODURO

CLUB: AZ
CURRENT RATING: 69
POTENTIAL RATING: 83

■ Having impressed at all age group levels, this Dutch goalkeeper is now in the first team at AZ in the Eredivisie. With excellent reflexes, his shot-stopping ability has already had scouts from bigger clubs flocking to watch him.

69 GK

Beadle

DIV	HAN	KIC	REF	SPD	POS
68	67	68	69	46	70

PLAYER: JAMES BEADLE

CLUB: SHEFFIELD WEDNESDAY
CURRENT RATING: 69
POTENTIAL RATING: 82

■ Born in London, **Beadle** has been capped for England from Under 15s right through to the Under 21s. He can be found playing in the Championship for Sheffield Wednesday on loan from Premier League Brighton.

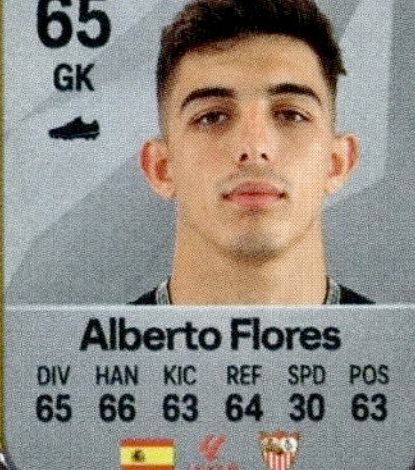

65 GK

Alberto Flores

DIV	HAN	KIC	REF	SPD	POS
65	66	63	63	30	63

PLAYER: ALBERTO FLORES

CLUB: SEVILLA
CURRENT RATING: 65
POTENTIAL RATING: 80

■ A product of Sevilla's youth academy, **Flores** has already made his senior debut in the Copa Del Rey. He's also already in possession of a European trophy winners medal having been part of the Sevilla squad that won the 2023 UEFA Europa League on penalties against Roma.

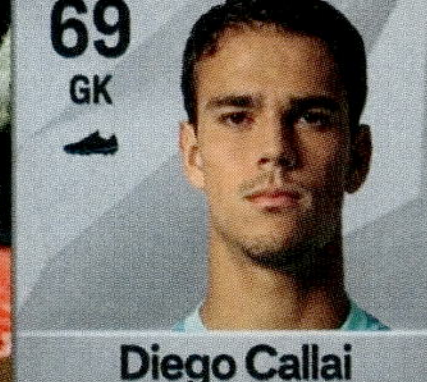

69 GK

Diego Callai

DIV	HAN	KIC	REF	SPD	POS
68	65	66	71	22	71

PLAYER: DIEGO CALLAI SILVA

CLUB: SPORTING
CURRENT RATING: 69
POTENTIAL RATING: 82

■ Born in Brazil, **Callai** is the son of a former goalkeeper. Now plying his trade in Portugal with Sporting, **Callai** holds Brazilian, Italian and Portuguese nationalities so could play for any of the three.

PLAYER: EWEN JAOUEN

66 GK

Jaouen

DIV	HAN	KIC	REF	SPD	POS
69	63	64	67	32	65

CLUB: USL DUNKERQUE
CURRENT RATING: 66
POTENTIAL RATING: 82

■ **Jaouen** can be found playing in Ligue 2 in France for USL Dunkerque where he is on loan from Ligue 1 club Stade de Reims. Standing at 6'6" tall with impressive diving ability, he can be a promising signing for the future.

PLAYER: ANDRÉ GOMES

65 GK

Andre Gomes

DIV	HAN	KIC	REF	SPD	POS
66	62	61	67	41	64

CLUB: BENFICA
CURRENT RATING: 65
POTENTIAL RATING: 81

■ **Gomes** is another starlet from Benfica, a club that's used to producing superstars! He's not tall for a goalkeeper, standing at only 6ft, but he's already showing progress across a number of skills and has a potential rating of 81.

PLAYER: MIKE PENDERS

65 GK

Penders

DIV	HAN	KIC	REF	SPD	POS
67	64	63	68	20	64

CLUB: GENK
CURRENT RATING: 65
POTENTIAL RATING: 83

■ Labelled the next **Thibaut Courtois**, this 6'7" Belgian giant has already been snapped up by Chelsea. Given the competition for places at Chelsea, it is possible that **Penders** could be an option in the loan market.

PLAYER: THOMAS GILLIER

63 GK

Gillier

DIV	HAN	KIC	REF	SPD	POS
64	58	60	67	21	63

CLUB: UNIVERSIDAD CATÓLICA
CURRENT RATING: 63
POTENTIAL RATING: 80

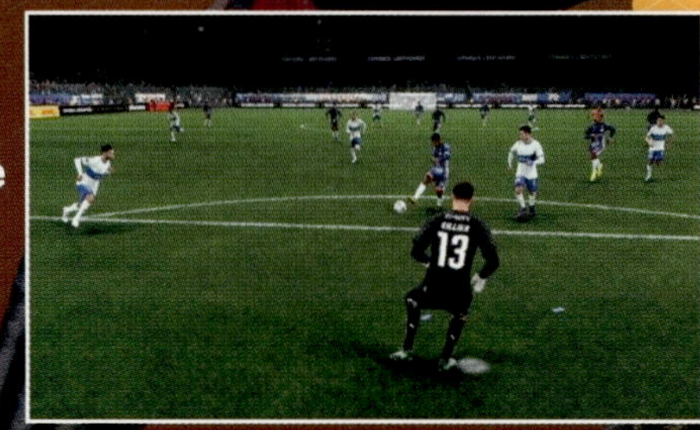

■ Born in 2004, **Gillier** is currently plying his trade in Chile. He's very much one for the future but already has impressive reflexes and a move to Europe may not be far away.

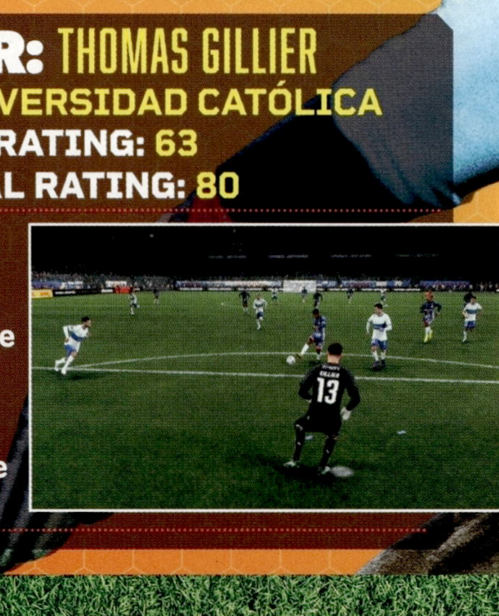

PLAYER: CHRIS BRADY
CLUB: CHICAGO FIRE
CURRENT RATING: 68
POTENTIAL RATING: 80

Brady initially played centre-back as a youngster before making a switch to goalkeeper and then becoming one of Major League Soccer's top prospects. Part of a strong crop of promising American players, **Brady** may follow **Gabriel Slonina** to Europe before too long.

PLAYER: GABRIEL SLONINA
CLUB: BARNSLEY
CURRENT RATING: 68
POTENTIAL RATING: 81

Born in the United States, **Slonina** is another one of Chelsea's many goalkeepers, signed for £10 million when only 18 years old. He's currently out on loan at Barnsley where he is already getting praise for his sweeper-keeper ability and impressive ball-playing skills.

Shutterstock (3)

Now it's time to look in front of the goalkeeper at some high-potential defensive talent!

DEFENDER WONDERKIDS

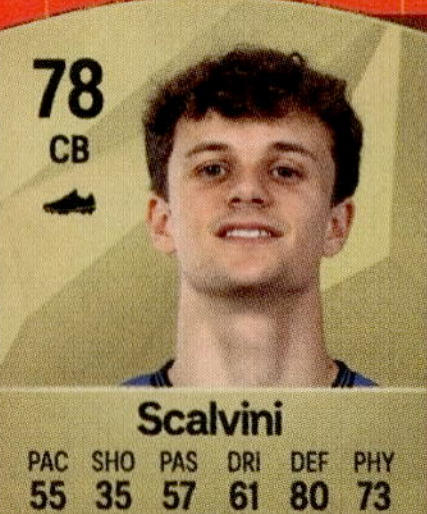

78
CB
Scalvini

PAC	SHO	PAS	DRI	DEF	PHY
55	35	57	61	80	73

PLAYER: GIORGIO SCALVINI
CLUB: ATLANTA
CURRENT RATING: 78
POTENTIAL RATING: 88

Scalvini made his debut for Atalanta aged 17 before being capped for Italy only two years later. The latest in a long line of outstanding Italian defenders, Scalvini has the potential to be the best of the best!

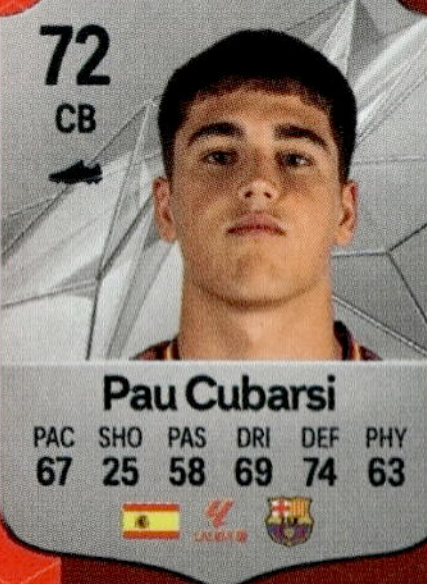

72
CB
Pau Cubarsi

PAC	SHO	PAS	DRI	DEF	PHY
67	25	58	69	74	63

PLAYER: PAU CUBARSÍ
CLUB: BARCELONA
CURRENT RATING: 72
POTENTIAL RATING: 88

Born in 2007, Cubarsí is one of the youngest of Barcelona's first-team wonderkids. He has already impressed with his passing ability, reading of the game and tackling ability.

PLAYER: LENY YORO

CLUB: MANCHESTER UNITED
CURRENT RATING: 78
POTENTIAL RATING: 86

	PAC	SHO	PAS	DRI	DEF	PHY
Yoro	73	41	59	61	79	73

■ **Yoro** signed for Manchester United in 2024 for £52 million, making him the most expensive player aged 18 or younger. He's already shown glimpses of his classy, elegant style and could be a key part of the United defence for many years to come.

PLAYER: HARRY AMASS

CLUB: MANCHESTER UNITED
CURRENT RATING: 60
POTENTIAL RATING: 85

	PAC	SHO	PAS	DRI	DEF	PHY
Amass	73	29	46	61	55	58

■ **Amass** is a tough-tackling England youth international who is working towards breaking into the first team at Manchester United. With a current rating of only 60, he has plenty of room to improve to a potential 85 rating.

PLAYER: JORREL HATO

CLUB: AJAX
CURRENT RATING: 73
POTENTIAL RATING: 88

	PAC	SHO	PAS	DRI	DEF	PHY
Hato	86	39	66	72	74	70

■ Left-footed **Hato** can play centre-back or left-back and has already made over 60 appearances for Dutch giants Ajax. As well as stopping attackers, he's also comfortable attacking forward with the ball.

PLAYER: ALEJANDRO BALDE

CLUB: BARCELONA
CURRENT RATING: 81
POTENTIAL RATING: 89

	PAC	SHO	PAS	DRI	DEF	PHY
Balde	91	48	73	78	75	64

■ Barcelona's young left-back is one of the many promising youngsters they now have in the first-team. **Balde** is attack-minded, not short of pace and great for those over-lapping runs!

PLAYER: ANTÓNIO SILVA

CLUB: BENFICA
CURRENT RATING: 79
POTENTIAL RATING: 87

Antonio Silva

PAC	SHO	PAS	DRI	DEF	PHY
80	37	64	69	79	80

■ **Silva** is already a first-team regular at Benfica as well as a regular for the Portuguese national team. Comfortable with both feet and a sound ability to read the game, he's tipped as a future Portugal captain.

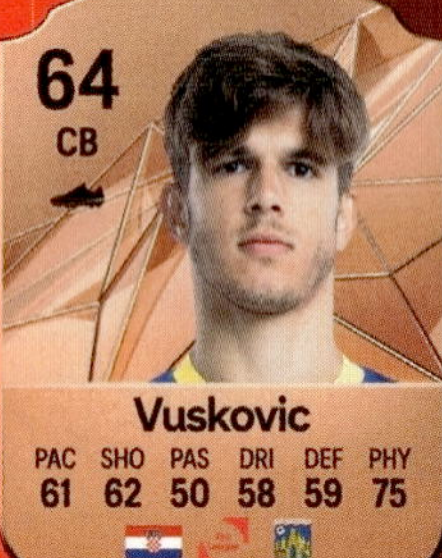

PLAYER: LUKA VUŠKOVIĆ

CLUB: WESTERLO
CURRENT RATING: 64
POTENTIAL RATING: 86

Vuskovic

PAC	SHO	PAS	DRI	DEF	PHY
61	62	50	58	59	75

■ **Vušković** is currently on loan in Belgium but will join Tottenham in the summer of 2025. Having made his debut in the Croatian league only two days after turning 16, he has shown promise from an early age.

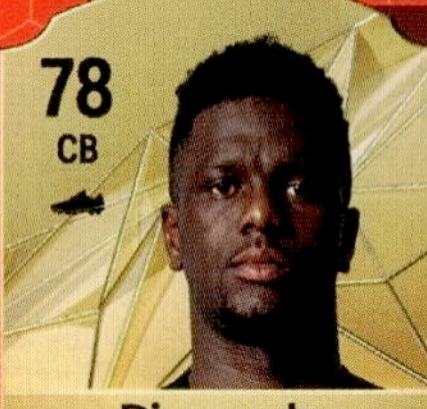

PLAYER: OUSMANE DIOMANDE

CLUB: SPORTING
CURRENT RATING: 78
POTENTIAL RATING: 86

Diomande

PAC	SHO	PAS	DRI	DEF	PHY
80	26	53	73	77	83

■ A right-sided defender with impressive physicality, vision and speed, **Diomande** impressed in Denmark before making a £6 million move to Sporting. Could the next stop be the Premier League?

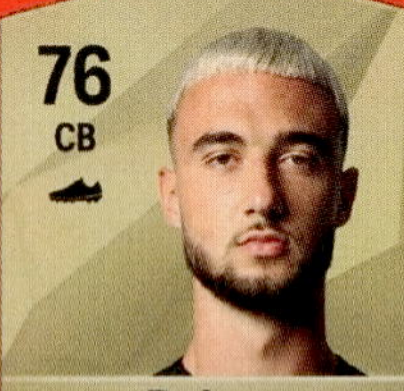

PLAYER: ZENO DEBAST

CLUB: SPORTING
CURRENT RATING: 76
POTENTIAL RATING: 86

Debast

PAC	SHO	PAS	DRI	DEF	PHY
66	53	71	72	76	76

■ Signed by Sporting from Anderlecht for £14 million plus add-ons and a 15% sell-on clause, **Debast** relishes defending, particularly in 1v1 situations where he excels.

65
CB

Jeltsch

PAC	SHO	PAS	DRI	DEF	PHY
66	36	51	57	65	69

PLAYER: FINN JELTSCH
CLUB: NÜRNBERG
CURRENT RATING: 65
POTENTIAL RATING: 84

Jeltsch is a good player to target given his low current rating and high potential ceiling. He has strong recovery pace and makes well-timed tackles.

77
CB

Mosquera

PAC	SHO	PAS	DRI	DEF	PHY
76	46	60	56	79	77

PLAYER: CRISTHIAN MOSQUERA
CLUB: VALENCIA
CURRENT RATING: 77
POTENTIAL RATING: 86

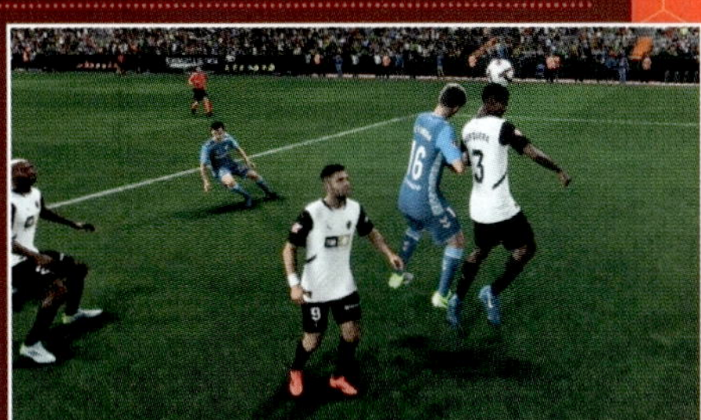

While Mosquera has predominantly played at centre-back, he can also play full-back on both sides. He has good anticipation skills, ball-playing ability and pace to go with it!

Shutterstock (3)

■ Now it's time to identify some major talent across the midfield area!

MIDFIELD WONDERKIDS

81
RW
RM
LW

Lamine Yamal

PAC	SHO	PAS	DRI	DEF	PHY
82	75	76	82	23	48

PLAYER: LAMINE YAMAL
CLUB: BARCELONA
CURRENT RATING: 81
POTENTIAL RATING: 94

■ Aged only six, Yamal was scouted by Barcelona and invited to train. Since then, he's gone on to become a first team regular, win La Liga and become a Euro 2024 champion with Spain. With fantastic passing ability, dribbling skills, pace and balance, there is nothing this guy can't do!

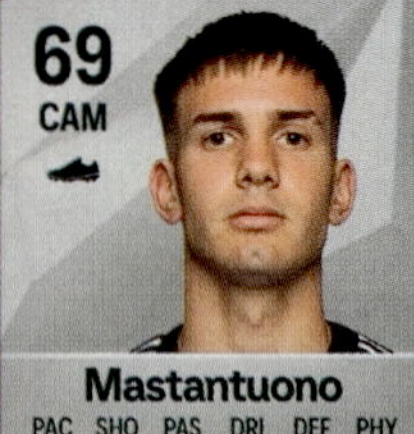

69
CAM

Mastantuono

PAC	SHO	PAS	DRI	DEF	PHY
75	62	67	72	48	63

PLAYER: FRANCO MASTANTUONO
CLUB: RIVER PLATE
CURRENT RATING: 69
POTENTIAL RATING: 87

■ This left-footed midfielder is already noted for his ball-striking ability. With low current stats and high potential rating, Mastantuono is a player worth trying to pick up in Career Mode.

71 CAM

Echeverri

PAC	SHO	PAS	DRI	DEF	PHY
87	62	67	79	35	44

PLAYER: CLAUDIO ECHEVERRI
CLUB: RIVER PLATE
CURRENT RATING: 71
POTENTIAL RATING: 87

With pace to burn and impressive dribbling skills, **Echeverri** has the potential to make a big impact with Manchester City whom he signed for in January 2024 before being loaned back to River Plate.

69 CAM · CM

Ouedraogo

PAC	SHO	PAS	DRI	DEF	PHY
77	56	60	76	45	69

PLAYER: ASSAN OUÉDRAOGO
CLUB: RB LEIPZIG
CURRENT RATING: 69
POTENTIAL RATING: 87

RB Leipzig splashed out nearly £9 million to sign this youngster when only 18 years old. A box-to-box midfielder, he's an imposing figure who can carry the ball well.

71 RM · LM · RW

Diao Diaoune

PAC	SHO	PAS	DRI	DEF	PHY
90	69	60	73	30	56

PLAYER: ASSANE DIAO DIAOUNE
CLUB: REAL BETIS
CURRENT RATING: 71
POTENTIAL RATING: 87

This young midfielder can play on either side and possesses explosive acceleration and sprint speed. With his shooting and dribbling skills sure to improve, he'll be a match for any defender.

72 CAM · CM · RW

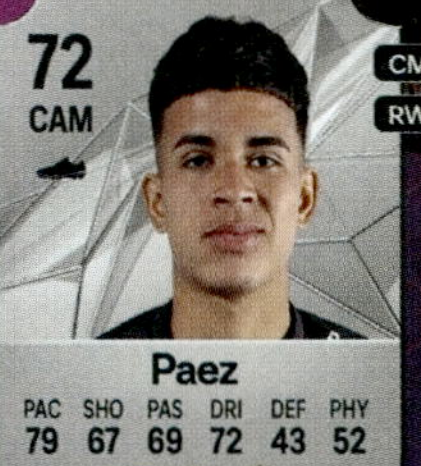

Paez

PAC	SHO	PAS	DRI	DEF	PHY
79	67	69	72	43	52

PLAYER: KENDRY PÁEZ
CLUB: INDEPENDIENTE DEL VALLE
CURRENT RATING: 72
POTENTIAL RATING: 87

This Ecuadorian wonderkid has already been snapped up by Chelsea and will join the club in 2025. Ideal in the number 10 role, **Páez** has good close control and is very skilled at spotting teammates' runs and playing through balls.

PLAYER: OSCAR GLOUKH

CLUB: RB SALZBURG
CURRENT RATING: 76
POTENTIAL RATING: 87

Gloukh is an Israeli attacking midfielder already being linked with the big Premier League clubs. With impressive composure, creativity and vision, **Gloukh** could be a playmaker you'll be hearing a lot more about in the coming years.

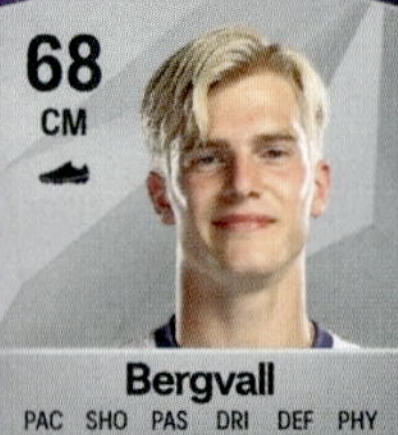

PLAYER: LUCAS BERGVALL

CLUB: TOTTENHAM
CURRENT RATING: 68
POTENTIAL RATING: 87

Swedish wonderkid **Bergvall** has settled in well to life at Tottenham. He's very comfortable on the ball and Spurs fans will be glad he rejected a move to Barcelona to sign for them.

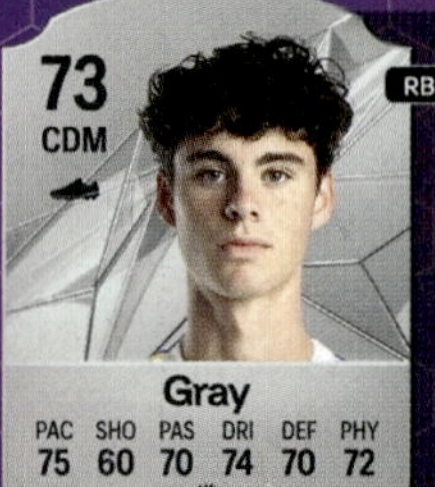

PLAYER: ARCHIE GRAY

CLUB: TOTTENHAM
CURRENT RATING: 73
POTENTIAL RATING: 87

Signed for £35 million from Leeds United, **Gray** is the 6th most expensive teenager in Premier League history. He has already impressed fans with his versatility across midfield and defence.

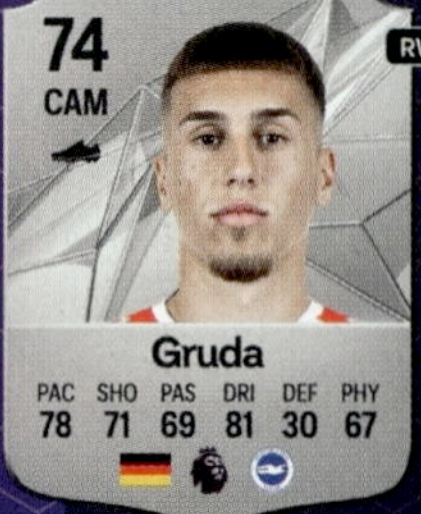

PLAYER: BRAJAN GRUDA

CLUB: BRIGHTON
CURRENT RATING: 74
POTENTIAL RATING: 87

Brighton have an impressive track record in signing talented young players and **Gruda** could be the next one to impress. He has strong dribbling skills and can be effective playing on either side.

PLAYER: GEOVANY QUENDA
CLUB: SPORTING
CURRENT RATING: 67
POTENTIAL RATING: 88

■ **Quenda** was playing Under-23 team football at Sporting aged only 16 and then made his full first-team debut at 17 under then coach Ruben Amorim. His high potential rating shows what he can become!

PLAYER: WARREN ZAÏRE-EMERY
CLUB: PARIS SAINT-GERMAIN
CURRENT RATING: 80
POTENTIAL RATING: 90

■ **Emery** is already a regular at Paris Saint-Germain thanks to his impressive all-round game. He can pass and shoot, get up and down the pitch easily and is no slouch defensively.

DID YOU KNOW?

When winger **Jadon Sancho** made his England debut in a game against Croatia in October 2018, he was the first player born in the 21st century to represent the country.

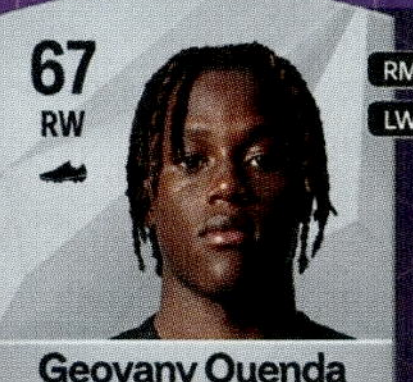

If it's goals you want, then look no further than these young hot-shots!

STRIKERS WONDERKIDS

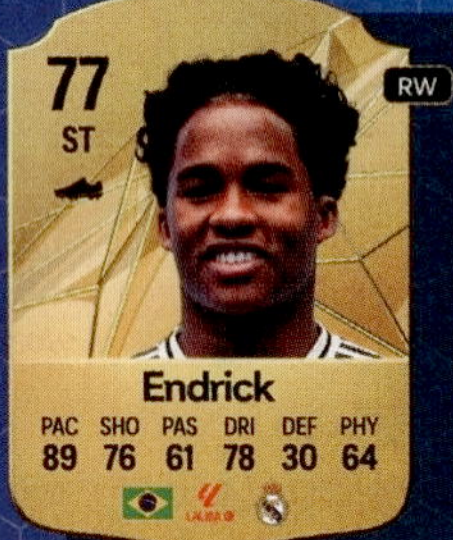

PLAYER: ENDRICK
CLUB: REAL MADRID
CURRENT RATING: 77
POTENTIAL RATING: 91

Endrick signed a six-year deal at Real Madrid in July 2024 and is hotly tipped as their next big superstar. He's the best young striker by a distance in **EA SPORTS FC 25** and is one everyone will want in their team.

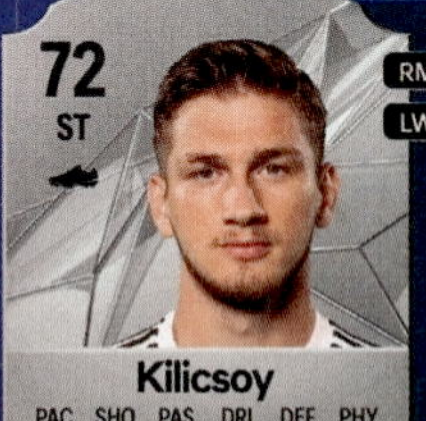

PLAYER: SEMIH KILIÇSOY
CLUB: BEŞIKTAŞ
CURRENT RATING: 72
POTENTIAL RATING: 88

With a high potential rating only three less than **Endrick, this Turkish youngster offers a potentially cheaper alternative. With decent finishing ability and flexibility to play across the attack, he is one to watch.

PLAYER: VITOR ROQUE

76 ST (RW / LW)

Vitor Roque

PAC 85 | SHO 79 | PAS 59 | DRI 80 | DEF 20 | PHY 64

CLUB: REAL BETIS
CURRENT RATING: 76
POTENTIAL RATING: 87

■ **Roque** signed for Barcelona in 2003 and was loaned out to Real Betis a season later. While his preferred role is striker, his pace and dribbling skills means he can also excel as a second striker or winger.

PLAYER: KARIM KONATÉ

73 ST

Konate

PAC 86 | SHO 70 | PAS 56 | DRI 75 | DEF 40 | PHY 65

CLUB: RB SALZBURG
CURRENT RATING: 73
POTENTIAL RATING: 87

■ **Konaté** has pace to burn and knows how to find the back of the net with ease. He has room for improvement with his technique but has time on his side to develop.

PLAYER: PARIS BRUNNER

65 ST (LM)

Brunner

PAC 68 | SHO 66 | PAS 51 | DRI 67 | DEF 27 | PHY 59

CLUB: CERCLE BRUGGE
CURRENT RATING: 65
POTENTIAL RATING: 87

■ **Brunner** left Dortmund to sign for Monaco before being loaned out to play in the Belgian Pro League. He first arrived on the radar of big clubs after scoring 16 goals in only five Under-17 Bundesliga appearances!

PLAYER: MUSTAFA ERHAN HEKIMOĞLU

62 ST (RW / LW)

Hekimoglu

PAC 64 | SHO 60 | PAS 50 | DRI 61 | DEF 27 | PHY 58

CLUB: BEŞİKTAŞ
CURRENT RATING: 62
POTENTIAL RATING: 86

■ **Hekimoğlu** is another promising young talent from Turkey with an impressive goal-scoring record at youth level. With plenty of room for improvement, he's worth trying to sign early.

PLAYER: MATHYS TEL

CLUB: BAYERN MUNICH
CURRENT RATING: 77
POTENTIAL RATING: 88

77 ST — RM LM

Tel

PAC	SHO	PAS	DRI	DEF	PHY
86	80	64	77	29	64

Tel's stats are already impressive enough to command a starting role in most clubs' first team. The French youngster has been compared to both Kylian Mbappé and Karim Benzema and is already well on his way to 100 appearances with Bayern Munich.

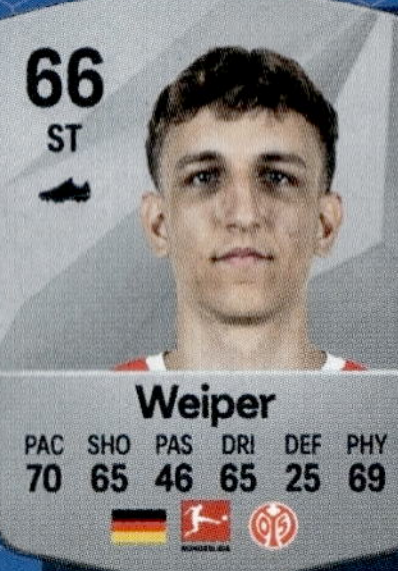

PLAYER: NELSON WEIPER

CLUB: MAINZ
CURRENT RATING: 66
POTENTIAL RATING: 85

66 ST

Weiper

PAC	SHO	PAS	DRI	DEF	PHY
70	65	46	65	25	69

Standing at 6'3", Weiper is an interesting striking option. Already a regular in the Bundesliga, he is a target man who can play with back-to-goal while also being willing to run in behind.

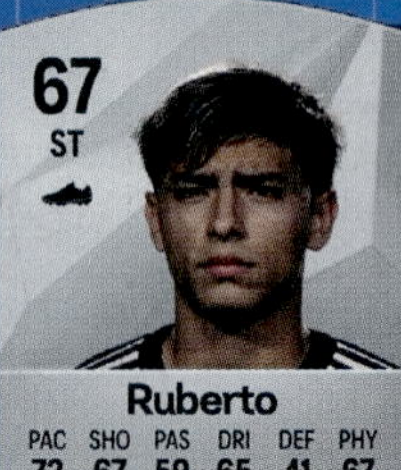

PLAYER: AGUSTÍN RUBERTO

CLUB: RIVER PLATE
CURRENT RATING: 67
POTENTIAL RATING: 83

67 ST

Ruberto

PAC	SHO	PAS	DRI	DEF	PHY
72	67	59	67	41	67

Ruberto is another potential young superstar to burst on the scene at River Plate. Top European clubs are already rumoured to be interested so you may have to act fast if you want to snap him up!

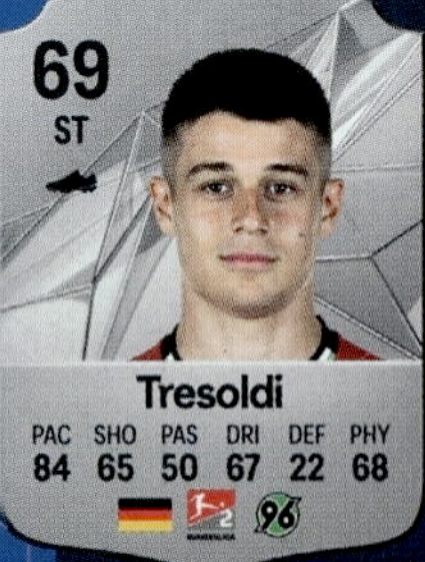

PLAYER: NICOLÒ TRESOLDI

CLUB: HANNOVER 96
CURRENT RATING: 69
POTENTIAL RATING: 83

69 ST

Tresoldi

PAC	SHO	PAS	DRI	DEF	PHY
84	65	50	67	22	68

Although born in Italy, Tresoldi has gone on to make his debut for Germany under-21s. Already a regular for Hannover 96 in Germany, Tresoldi is physical with impressive speed.

DID YOU KNOW?

When it comes to strikers scoring goals, Pele, the Brazilian soccer legend, is the man to beat given he holds the career record with 1,281 goals in 1,363 games!

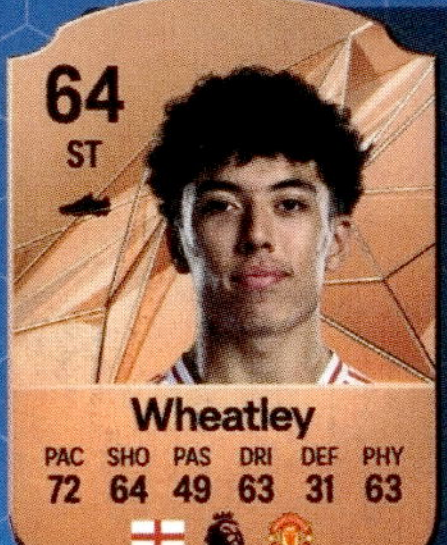

PLAYER: ETHAN WHEATLEY

CLUB: MANCHESTER UNITED
CURRENT RATING: 64
POTENTIAL RATING: 83

Wheatley has made his debut for Manchester United's first team and is one of their many promising youngsters currently on the books. He can score all types of goals thanks to his impressive touch and clever movement.

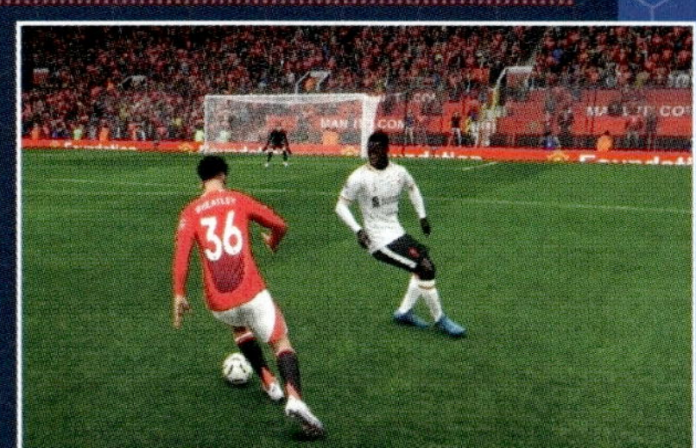

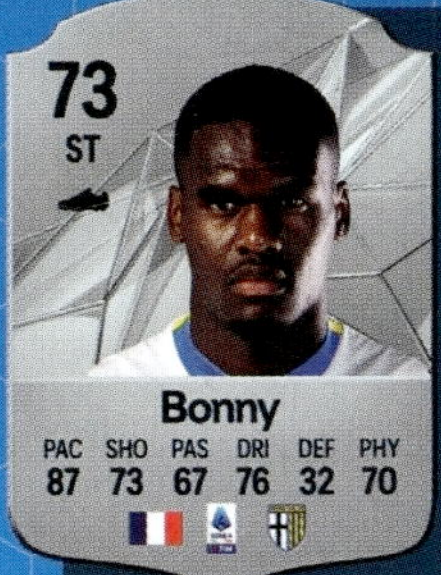

PLAYER: ANGE-YOAN BONNY

CLUB: PARMA
CURRENT RATING: 73
POTENTIAL RATING: 83

Bonny is playing in Serie A with Parma and is already a regular in their first team. He is right-footed, has a ton of speed and has decent finishing ability.

Shutterstock (3)

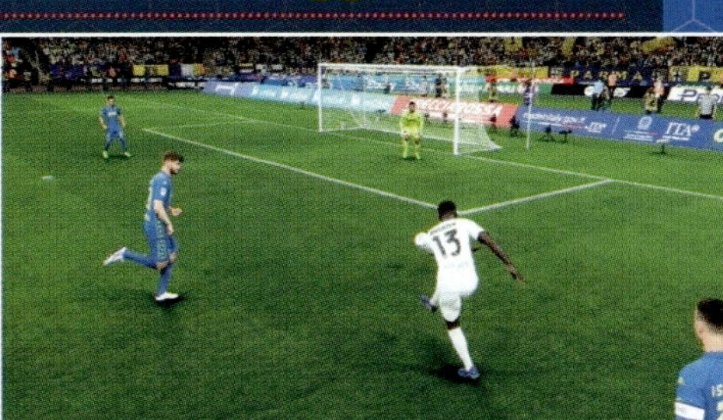

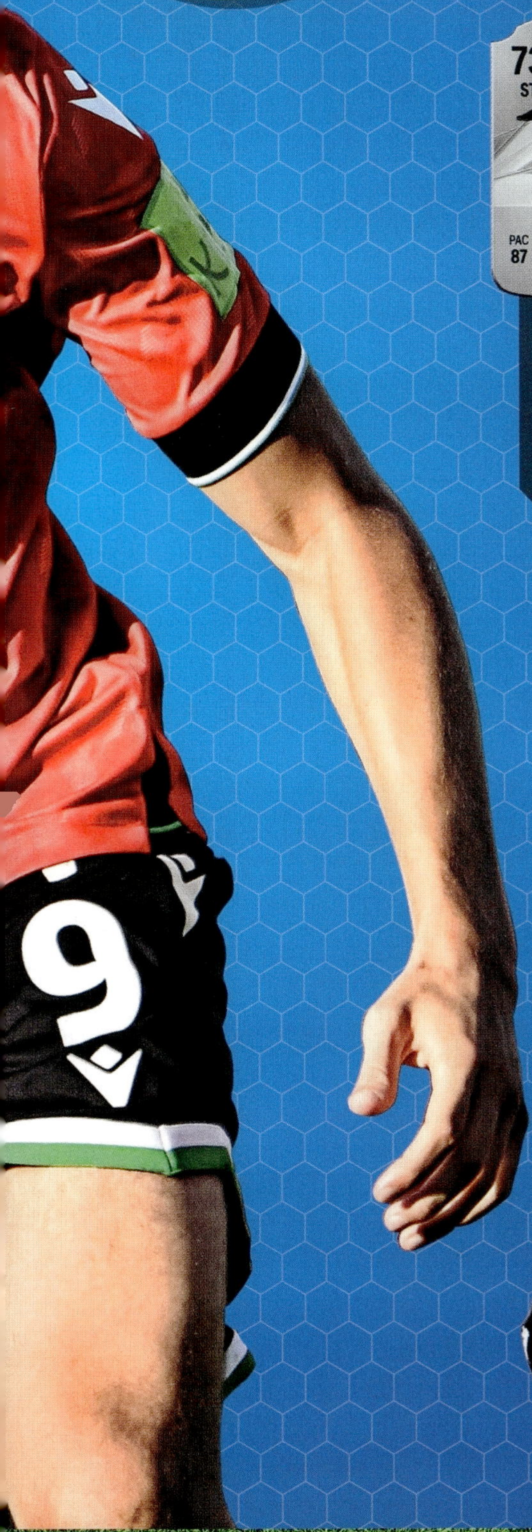

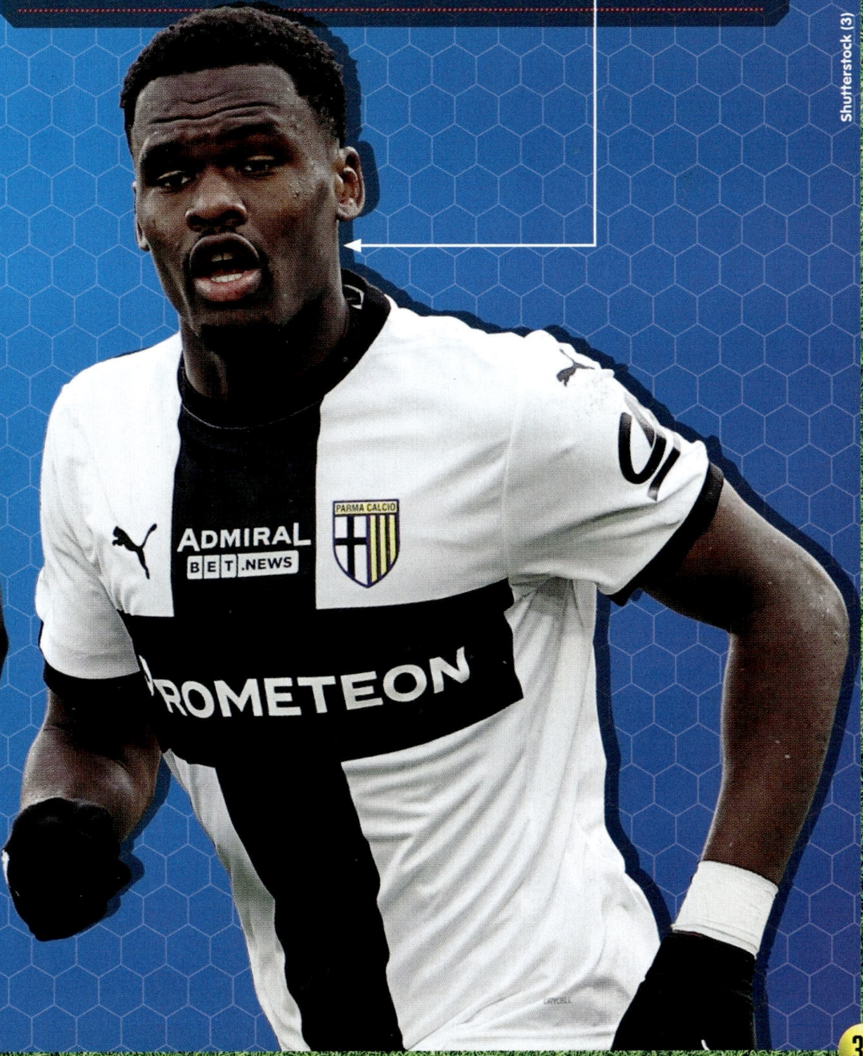

8 STAGES OF LOSING AT EA SPORTS FC25

STAGE 1

SCORE: 0 - 0

CONFIDENCE

- You're the FC 25 master, you've got this match in the bag – GAME ON!

STAGE 2

SCORE: 0 - 1

DETERMINATION

- One-nil down, that's nothing. You can come back from this. Easy!

STAGE 3

SCORE: 0 - 2

PANIC

- You're on the edge of your seat, leaning closer to the screen and making all the subs!

STAGE 4

SCORE: 0 - 3

ANGER

- MUST. NOT. RAGE. QUIT. You've entered the controller danger zone, no-one is safe.

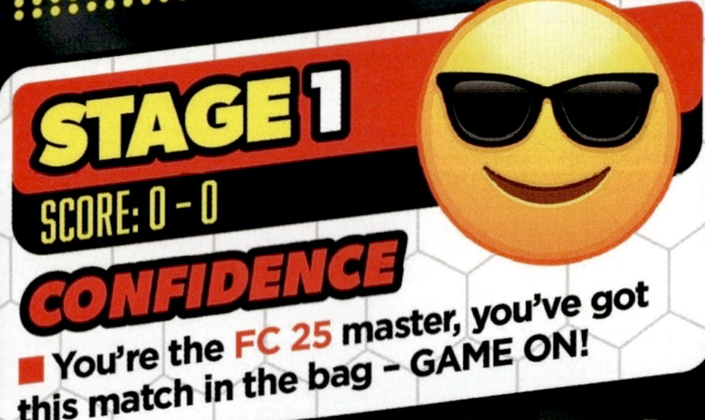

LOSE LIKE A WINNER!

VLA

STAGE 5
SCORE: 0 - 4
SADNESS
You're not being dramatic, but this is literally the worst thing to have happened to anyone EVER!

STAGE 6
SCORE: 0 - 5
EXCUSES
It's not your fault. You'd be winning if they weren't cheating. Or the ref wasn't blind. Or the game wasn't glitching.

STAGE 7
SCORE: 1 - 5
HOPE
YAAAAS! YOU CAN DO THIS. THERE'S STILL TIME. THE COMEBACK IS ON!

STAGE 8
SCORE: 1 - 5
ACCEPTANCE
It's OK to lose. The better player won and that's cool.

Pics: Shutterstock (2)

TOP

GAMER TIPS
EA SPORTS FC25

ALL-ROUND
4-1-2-1-2

If you're not sure what type of player you are, or you just want a solid team on the pitch, the best and most popular formation is this diamond shape!

BEST BEGINNER PICK!

ATTACKING
3-4-2-1

For the team that loves all out attack. This team is a bit risky at the back, but it makes up for it with its aggressive play!

DEFENSIVE
5-3-2

If you're being picked apart by pacey strikers, the 5-3-2 formation will give you great coverage. Overwhelm your rivals with defence.

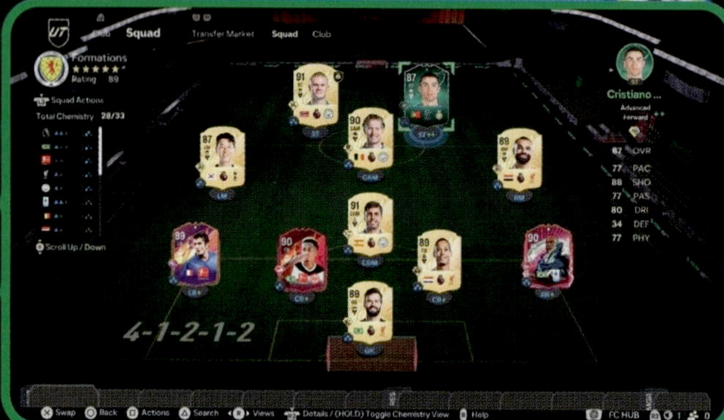

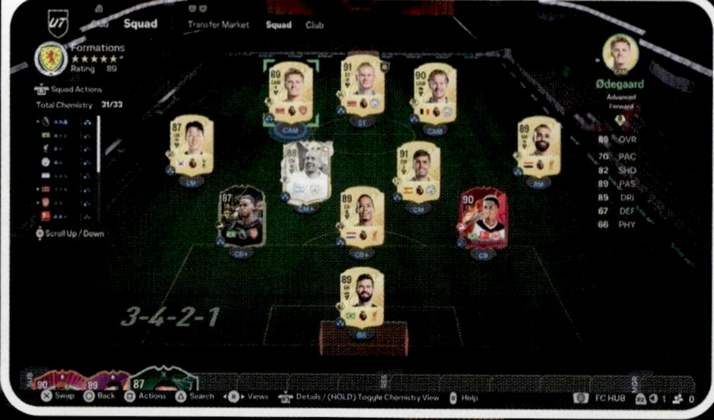

COUNTER ATTACK
5-2-1-2

■ This formation is solid at the back, making it hard for your opponents to score. And is ideal for a quick break up the pitch!

POSSESSION
4-5-1

■ Love keeping the ball? This formation is perfect for players who love to pass it around until the other team makes a mistake!

CROSSING
3-4-3

■ Whipping in dangerous balls and heading home a winner is always a satisfying way to score. Defending against a skilled crossing team is tough!

COLD
Hold L2/LT
+ R/RS Spin
right to left

LETS
CELEBRATE

Okay, so you've hit the
back of the net but how will
you celebrate? Check out
these options!

THE SALUTE

YOGA

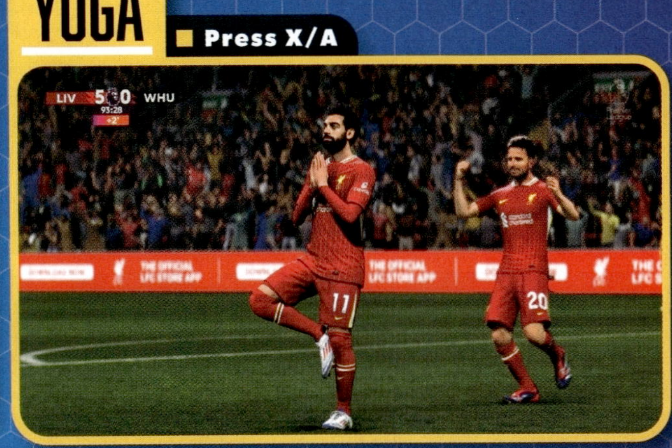

ARMS TO CROWD

THINK

HEART SYMBOL

DARTS

LITTLE BROTHER

CREATE YOUR OWN!

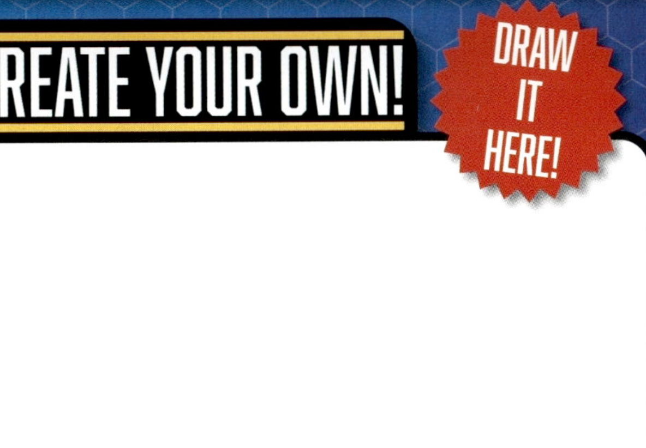

DRAW IT HERE!

POWER PROFILE!

JUDE BELLINGHAM

POWER UP!

Jude's energy is second to none! He can nip all over the field, running forward to score goals effortlessly and darting back to defend. His unpredictability and speed make it hard for the other team to even mark him properly!

DAMAGE ALERT!

There's a fear this wonderkid might try to do too much himself, leaving his teammates in the dust... and missing opportunities for co-operative play that just might be the difference between a W and an L for his team.

DID YOU KNOW?

⭐ Football runs in the family! Jude's dad Mark Bellingham was a non-league footballer, scoring over 700 goals in his career.

⭐ At 16 years and 38 days, he was the youngest player to start an English league for Birmingham City.

⭐ His transfer to Borussia Dortmund made him the most expensive 17-year-old in history, reported to have been around £25 million!

⭐ He's the cover star of EA SPORTS FC 25. He's the top of the table for the Intercept, Slide Tackle and Technical abilities, and the fifth highest ranked player overall.

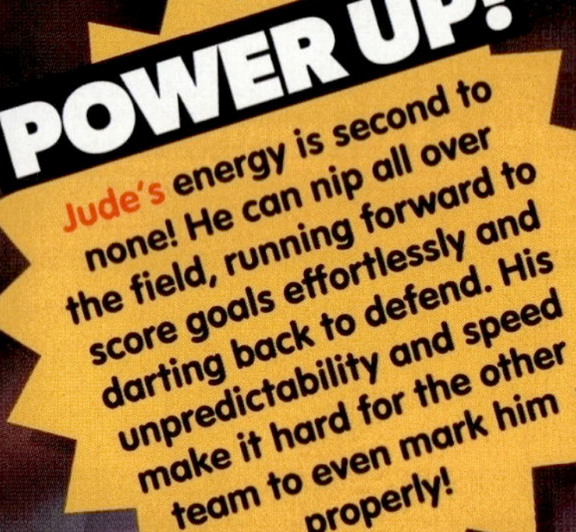

⭐ Birmingham City retired his famous #22 shirt when he left them – an honour usually reserved for footy icons!

STATS:

BORN:	29/06/2003
AGE:	21
POSITION:	ATTACKING MIDFIELDER
CLUBS:	BIRMINGHAM CITY, BORUSSIA DORTMUND, REAL MADRID
CLUB APPEARANCES:	235
GOALS:	54
NATIONAL TEAM:	ENGLAND
INT CAPS:	40
INT GOALS:	6

GOING FOR GOLD
BEAT THIS MAZE TO MAKE IT TO FOOTBALL GLORY!
START
FINISH
JOKE ALERT!
WHAT POSITION DO GHOSTS PLAY?
GHOULIE!
ANSWER
START
FINISH
Shutterstock (1)
43

Pics: Shutterstock (8)

WHO SCORED THE MOST SOCCER GOALS IN THE GREEK MYTHOLOGY LEAGUE?
THE CENTAUR FORWARD!
WHICH FOOTBALL TEAM LOVES ICE-CREAM?
ASTON VANILLA!
WHY AREN'T FOOTBALL STADIUMS BUILT IN OUTER SPACE?
THEY NEED A LITTLE ATMOSPHERE!
WHY WAS THE FOOTBALL TEAM GREAT AT MUSIC?
THEY HAD THE BEST SCORES!
WHERE DO FOOTBALLERS GO TO DANCE?
THE FOOTBALL!
WHICH FOOTBALL TEAM DO COWBOYS SUPPORT?
SPURS!
WHICH FOOTBALL PLAYER ALWAYS LEAVES THEIR KIT ON THE FLOOR?
MESSI!
WHY WAS THE FOOTBALL PITCH WET?
THE PLAYERS HAD DRIBBLED ALL OVER IT!
WHAT'S A FOOTBALLER'S FAVOURITE PRECIOUS METAL?
GOOOOOLD!
WHAT FOOTBALL CLUB DO SHEEP SUPPORT?
BAAARCELONA!

TOP 10 CHAMPIONS LEAGUE WINNERS!

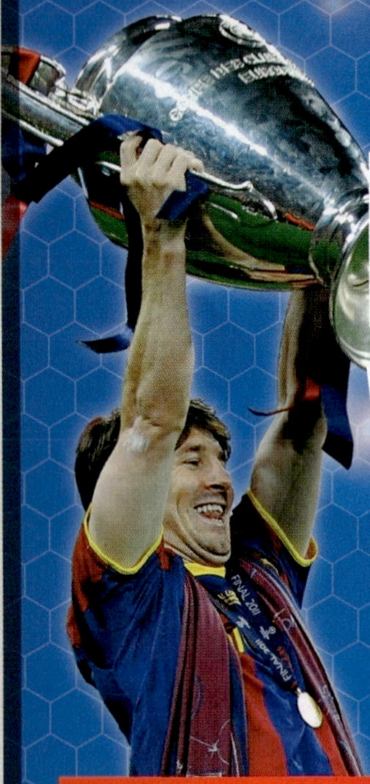

Once known as the European Cup, the tournament was given a different name in 1992 – the UEFA Champions League. Here we rank ten of the best winners!

10 REAL MADRID (2002)

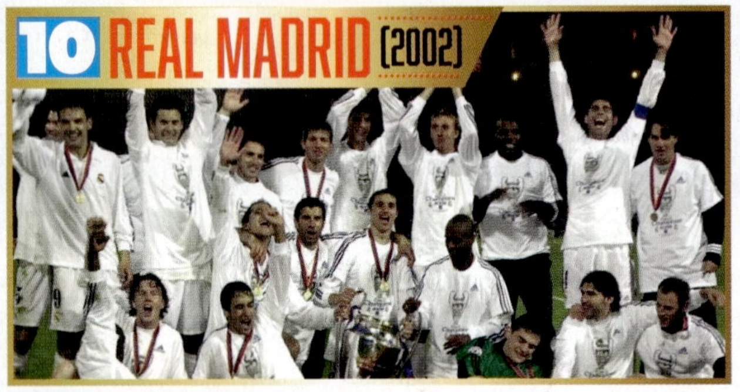

With Zinedine Zidane joining Raùl, Roberto Carlos and Luís Figo in the Real Madrid line-up, much was expected of this team. They scored 27 goals in 12 matches over two group stages and defeated Barcelona 2-0 at the Camp Nou in the semis. The final at Hampden Park saw one of the all-time great goals as Zidane volleyed a ball from the heavens into the back of the net.

9 AJAX (1995)

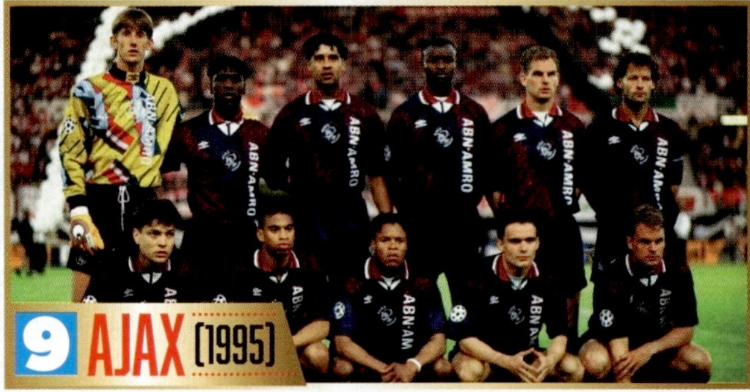

AC Milan were considered the strongest team in the world at the time, but this impressive young Ajax team beat them three times in the same competition. Twice in the group stage and again in the final. Led by veteran Frank Rijkaard, the young supporting cast of Davids, Seedorf, Overmars and Kluivert lit up the competition and ensured they lifted their fourth European Cup.

8 BAYERN MUNICH (2013)

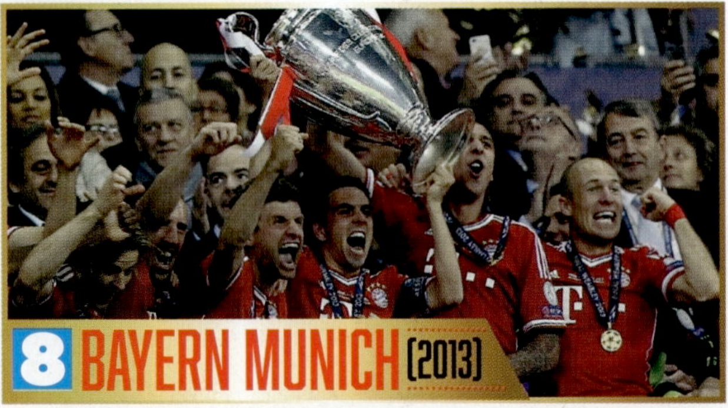

Half of this team went on to play in the 2014 World Cup final which highlights how strong it was. With the outstanding Franck Ribéry on one wing and Arjen Robben on the other, they easily beat Juventus 4-0 in the quarter-finals before spanking Barcelona 7-0 over two semi-final legs. A late winner over German rivals Dortmund secured the trophy.

7 REAL MADRID (2018)

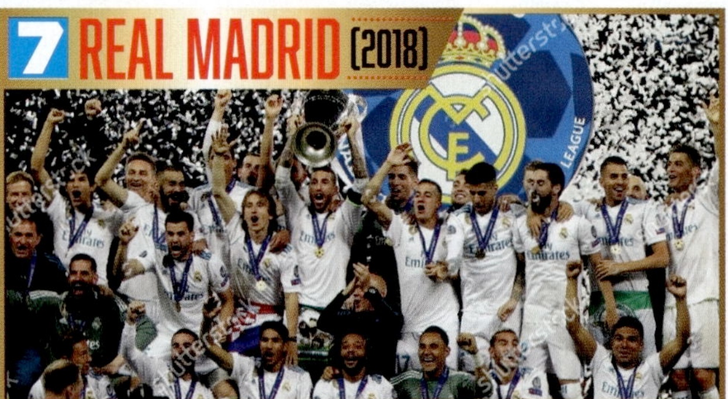

This win made it three Champions League triumphs in-a-row and will be remembered for two extraordinary goals – a Cristiano Ronaldo overhead kick against future club Juventus and Gareth Bale's amazing winner in the final against Liverpool. Along the way they also knocked out PSG and Bayern Munich, a run to the final as hard as could be.

6 BARCELONA (2015)

■ MSN – **Lionel Messi**, **Luis Suárez** and **Neymar** – were all on show scoring a combined 137 goals across 2015. This special team defeated the champions of England (Manchester City), the champions of France (PSG) and the champions of Germany (Bayern Munich) before toppling the champions of Italy (Juventus) in the final.

5 BARCELONA (2011)

■ **Lionel Messi** scored a remarkable 12 goals in the competition, including a double against Real Madrid at the Santiago Bernabeu in the semi-finals. With **David Villa** also enjoying a strong season up front and **Xavi** and **Iniesta** dictating play from midfield, Manchester United never stood a chance in the final and were comfortably beat 3-1 at Wembley.

4 BAYERN MUNICH (2020)

■ This win was peak Bayern Munich as they won six out of six in the group stage scoring 24 goals in the process. In the last 16 they put seven past Chelsea over two legs before beating Barcelona 8-2 in a one-off quarter-final. A straightforward 3-0 win followed over Lyon in the semis before beating PSG 1-0 in the final, meaning they'd lifted the trophy by winning every match along the way.

3 MANCHESTER UNITED (1999)

■ This win was the most incredible in Champions League history. Having already won the Premier League by one point followed by an FA Cup win over Newcastle, **Sir Alex Ferguson's** men travelled to the Camp Nou to face Bayern Munich in the final. They trailed 1-0 as the clock struck 90 minutes, only to go and score two injury-time goals and snatch the trophy from Bayern's grasp.

2 REAL MADRID (2017)

■ With **Cristiano Ronaldo**, **Karim Benzema** and **Gareth Bale** leading the line, and the likes of **Kroos**, **Modrić** and **Sergio Ramos** behind them, this Real team won La Liga, the UEFA Super Cup, Club World Cup and Champions League all in the same season. The latter was won by dismantling a strong Juventus team 4-1 in the final.

1 BARCELONA (2009)

■ The 2008/09 Barcelona team was perfection on a football pitch. A side with **Xavi**, **Iniesta**, **Busquets**, **Yaya Touré**, **Samuel Eto'o**, **Thierry Henry** and a young **Lionel Messi** were frighteningly good, seeing off Bayern Munich and then Chelsea before a comfortable 2-0 win over Manchester United in the final.

POWER PROFILE!

ERLING HAALAND

POWER UP!

Haaland is a true goal getter and is capable of scoring a variety of goals off either foot! His height, strength and speed make him a tough opponent for any defence.

DAMAGE ALERT!

He's incredible at scoring goals, but he could be more involved in the build-up play. He often focuses on getting into scoring positions, meaning he doesn't always link up with teammates early enough in the attack.

DID YOU KNOW?

⭐ His dad, **Alf-Inge Haaland**, played for Leeds when **Erling** was born, later captaining Manchester City – an influence on **Erling's** move from Borussia Dortmund!

⭐ He broke the record for the most Premier League goals scored in a single season with an impressive 36 goals!

⭐ He was the cover star for **EA SPORTS FC 24** and is one of the most valuable players in the game!

⭐ He scored eight hat-tricks in 69 Premier League games – on average that's one every nine games!

STATS:

BORN: 21/07/2000

AGE: 24

POSITION: CENTRE-FORWARD

CLUBS: SALZBURG, BORUSSIA DORTMUND, MANCHESTER CITY

CLUB APPEARANCES: 125

GOALS: 111

NATIONAL TEAM: NORWAY

INT CAPS: 39

INT GOALS: 38

Pics: Shutterstock (1) Stats correct at time of print

GROUP STAGE GRID!

CAN YOU FIND ALL EIGHT COUNTRIES HIDDEN IN THE GRID BELOW?

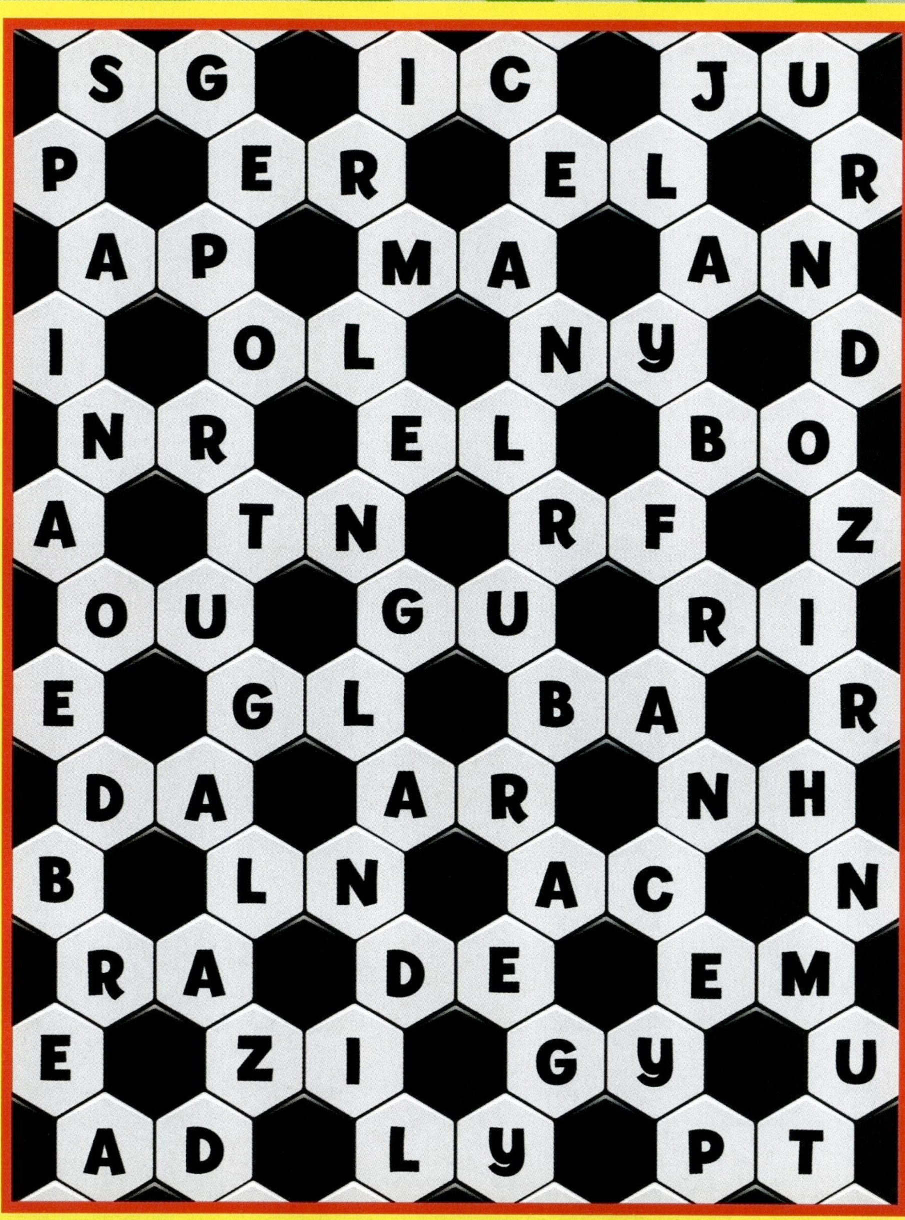

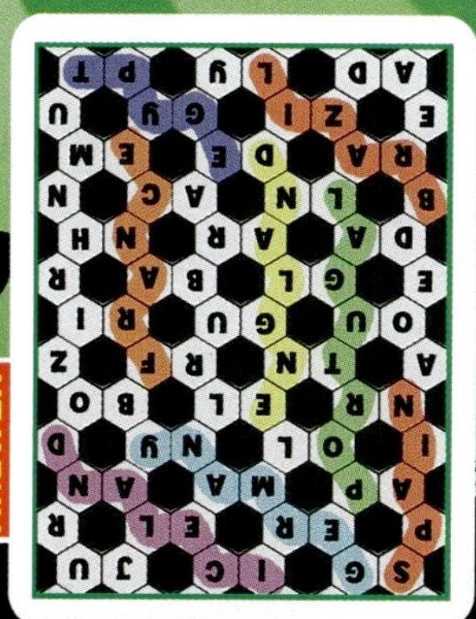

GET THE GOAL!

BATTLE IT OUT ON THE PITCH!

ALL YOU NEED:
★ A dice
★ Coins or buttons to use as counters

WHAT TO DO:
★ Each player starts at opposite ends of the board — one from space 1 and one from space 36.
★ Take turns to roll the dice to decide how many spaces you'll move, and follow the instructions on the space you land on.
★ The first player to reach the opposite end of the board wins!

START
P1 START HERE!

1

2

3
OFFSIDE! GO BACK ONE SPACE.

4
On the attack! Move forward three spaces.

5

6
YELLOW CARD! MISS A TURN.

7

8
Ball goes out of play. Stay where you are!

9

11

12

13
Lost possession! Move backward two spaces.

14

15
HALF TIME! PLAYERS SWAP DIRECTIONS ON THE BOARD!

16

17
GOOD PASS! MOVE FORWARD TWO SPACES.

19

BACK O' THE NET!
Substitutions! Roll the dice again.
FREE KICK! Move forward three spaces.
VAR check. Stay where you are!
PENALTY KICK! MOVE FORWARD THREE SPACES.
Corner! Move forward one space.
FOUL! MISS A TURN.
Injury! Move backward a space.
START
P2 START HERE!
PITCH PERFECT!
10
22
20
23
21
32
24
31
33
29
30
25
28
34
27
36
35
26
Shutterstock (1)
51

FANTASY FOOTBALL

TIPS & TRICKS!

As a fantasy manager, your mission is to choose a squad of real-life players who score points based on their performances each week. With a strategic selection of players, formations, and captains, you'll compete for points and prizes throughout the season.

BUILD A SQUAD

Armed with a budget of £100 million, it's your job to put together a squad of 15 players consisting of two goalkeepers, five defenders, five midfielders and three forwards. A maximum of three players may be selected from any one club.

HOW TO SCORE

Points are awarded to players for goals, assists, saves and clean sheets. There are additional bonus points available for players who have excelled in a match. Managers also choose a captain and a vice-captain for each game week. A captain's score is doubled, but if he doesn't play, then it's the vice-captain who scores double instead.

LEAGUES

When you join **Fantasy Premier League**, you'll be placed into various leagues, like a fan league for your favourite team and a country league. You can also create a mini-league to challenge your friends.

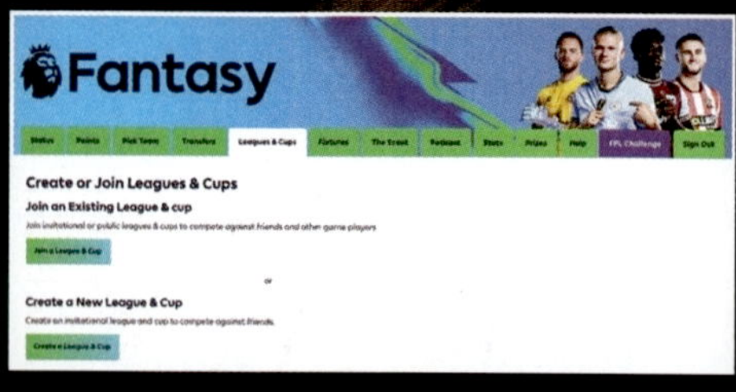

CHIPS

There are five chips to play over the course of the season which can boost your team's points total in a Gameweek... but you can only use one per Gameweek:

■ **Wildcard** – Completely change your team without forfeiting points (you have two Wildcards to use per season).

■ **Triple Captain** – Activating this chip means your captain gets three times their points total instead of the usual double.

■ **Bench Boost** – This chip lets you earn points from your non-playing substitutes, giving you 15 scoring players.

■ **Free Hit** – Reset your team by picking a new team for one week only before it reverts back to your original squad.

■ **The Assistant Manager Chip** – This new chip allows you to add a manager to your team to score points for three consecutive gameweeks. This real-life PL manager you add will score points for you if the PL team they manage picks up results.

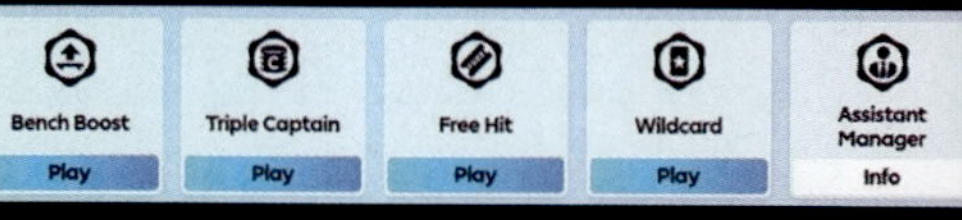

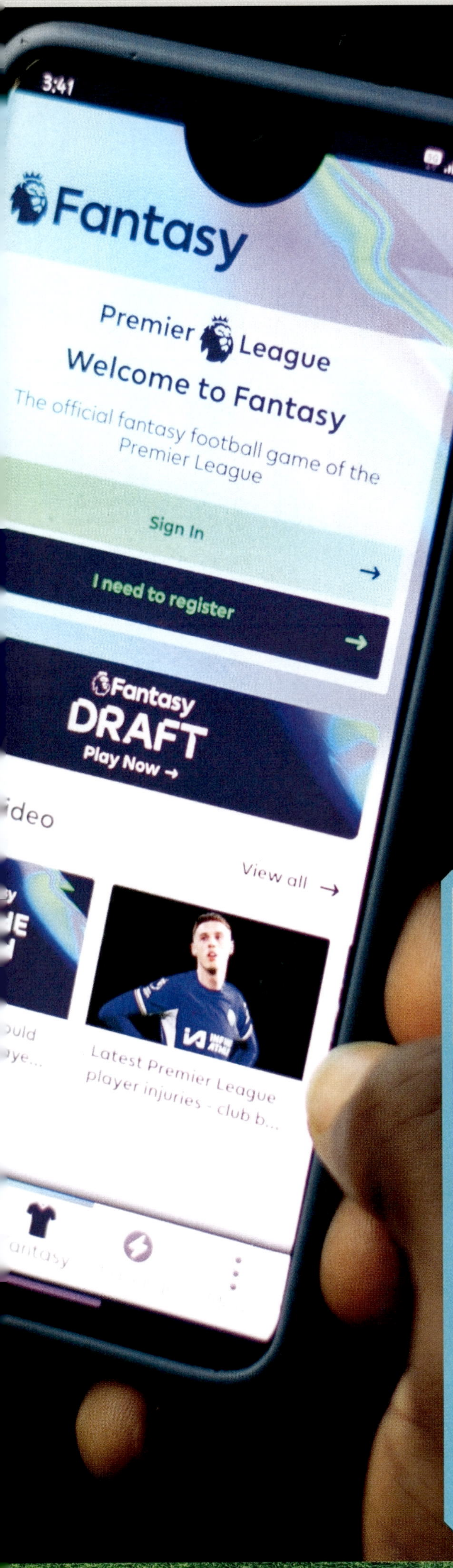

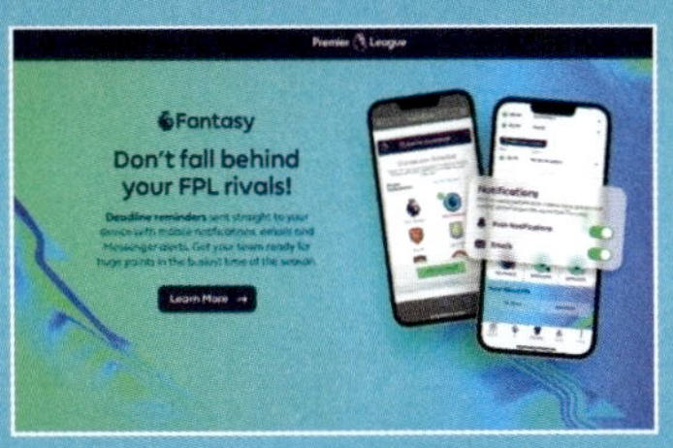

SAY MY NAME!

Being a **Fantasy Premier League** manager also allows you to choose your own team kit and team name. Some game managers like to try funny team names that incorporate real-life players. Check out some of the hilarious efforts!

- Dude Where's Micah?
- Alisson Wonderland
- Stranger Mings
- Major League Saka
- Thomas The Frank Engine
- Back of the Neto
- Eze Come Eze Go
- Tesco McNeil Deal
- The Konate Kid
- Onana, What's My Name?
- How Dalot Can You Go
- Burn Baby Burn
- Paqueta Crisps
- Bad to the Bowen
- Cunha Get Any Worse?

TOP 3 TIPS

1 Keep up-to-date with injuries, suspensions and fixtures. If you don't, you risk signing players who can't play or starting players who may have a tough match against a top team away from home.

2 Find the bargains! A £100 million budget may seem a lot but it's not enough to fill your squad full of elite players. Instead, you'll need to find six or seven lower cost bargains to fill your 15-man squad. How well these guys score will be key to a high finish.

3 Use your chips wisely. Some Gameweeks will see some teams play more than once. Especially if they had games postponed earlier in the season or have had good cup runs. If you have players in a team that are playing twice, then they'd make a good option to include in your Free Hit team or make a Triple Captain as they'll have two games to play meaning double the chance to score points!

FOOTBALL FUN ZONE

WARPED WONDERS

These footballers' faces have been pixelated! Match the player to their name.

FACT OR FIB?

Put your knowledge to the test and work out whether the statements are true or false!

T F

A) England won the World Cup in 1966.

B) Bayern Munich have won the most Champions League titles.

C) There are 18 teams in the Premier League.

T F

D) Manchester City won the Premier League in the 2023/24 season.

E) Arsenal have never won the FA Cup.

F) Alan Shearer is the all time top goal scorer in Premier League history.

MATCH MIX UP

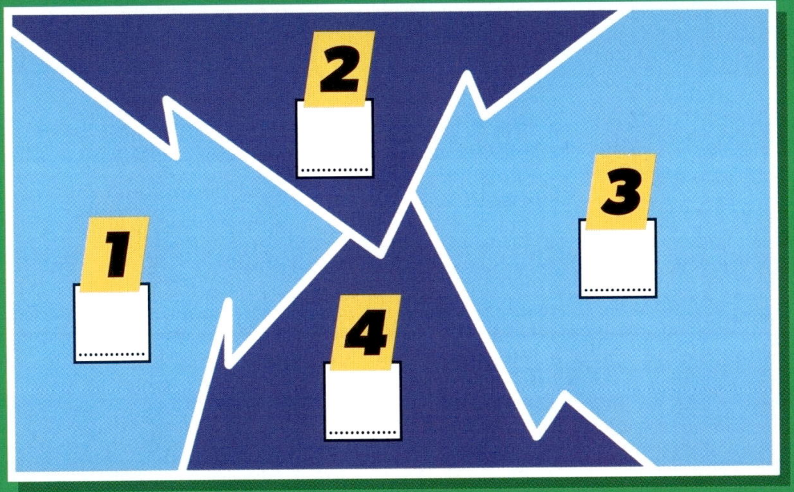

BUSY BOOTS

How many times can you count Barcelona superstar **Bonmatí** on the pitch?

GOAL GETTERS

Which team is celebrating a goal here?

☑ Borussia Dortmund ☑ Villarreal
☑ Paris Saint-Germain ☑ Juventus

Pics: Shutterstock (6)

ANSWERS:

WARPED WONDERS
1) Kane 2) Maguire
3) Salah 4) De Bruyne
5) Havertz

MATCH MIX UP
1) A, 2) D, 3) B, 4) C

BUSY BOOTS
19

FACT OR FIB
GOAL GETTERS
A) True B) False C) False Borussia Dortmund
D) True E) True F) True

FC25 PERFECT PLAYLIST

Tick your favourite tunes!

MATCH BUILD UP

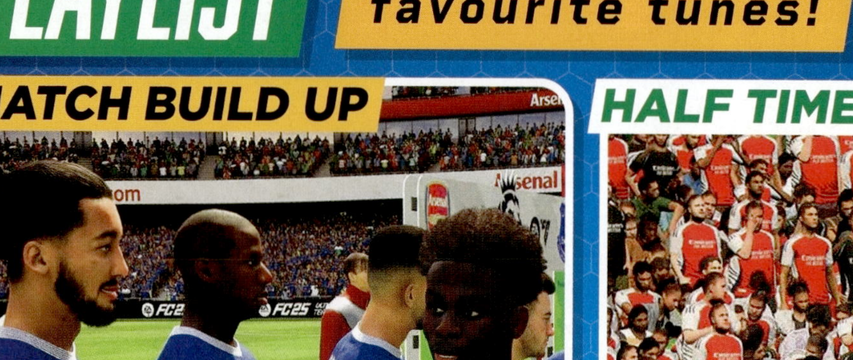

- ✔ **Thunderstruck - AC/DC**
- ✔ **Can't Hold Us - Macklemore and Ryan Lewis**
- ✔ **Seven Nation Army - The White Stripes**
- ✔ **I'm Good (Blue) - David Guetta and Bebe Rexha**

HALF TIME

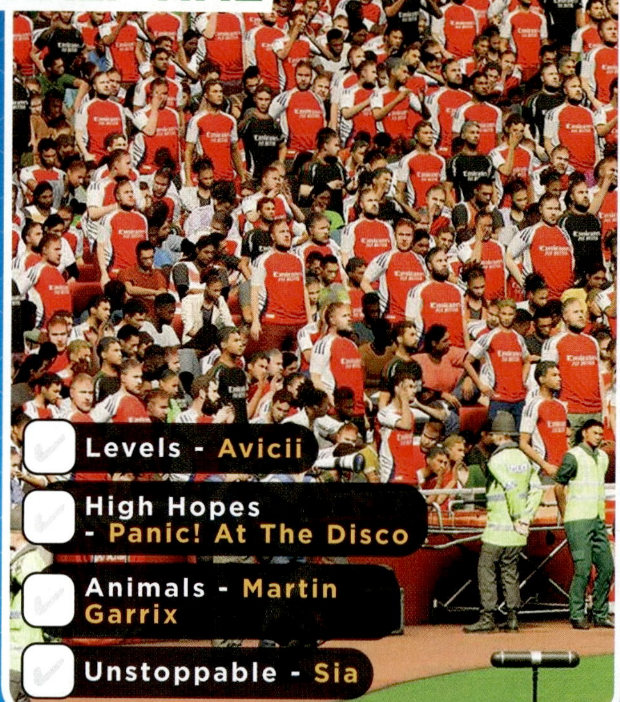

- ✔ **Levels - Avicii**
- ✔ **High Hopes - Panic! At The Disco**
- ✔ **Animals - Martin Garrix**
- ✔ **Unstoppable - Sia**

SCORING A GOAL

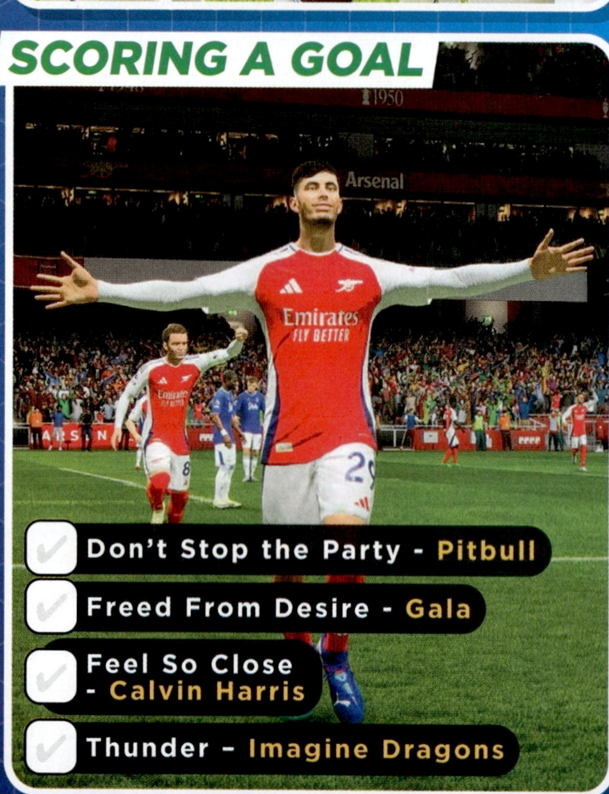

- ✔ **Don't Stop the Party - Pitbull**
- ✔ **Freed From Desire - Gala**
- ✔ **Feel So Close - Calvin Harris**
- ✔ **Thunder – Imagine Dragons**

FULL TIME

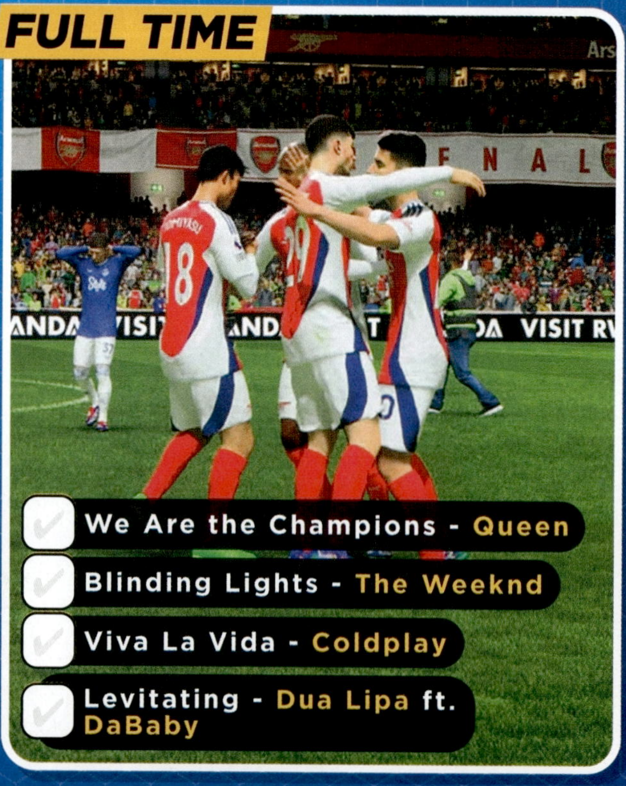

- ✔ **We Are the Champions - Queen**
- ✔ **Blinding Lights - The Weeknd**
- ✔ **Viva La Vida - Coldplay**
- ✔ **Levitating - Dua Lipa ft. DaBaby**

POWER PROFILE!

CRISTIANO RONALDO

POWER UP!

Considered the best of his generation with exceptional finishing ability, CR7 was the first-ever men's player to score an incredible 900 career goals in officially sanctioned matches!

DAMAGE ALERT!

On occasion, Ronaldo has been criticised for not always being a team player and has sometimes been known to exaggerate a foul when tackled. Oops!

DID YOU KNOW?

⭐ Ronaldo is the recipient of an impressive five Ballon d'Or awards!

⭐ Despite being famous as a forward, Ronaldo started out as a right-winger!

⭐ Cristiano helped Portugal pick up their first major international title at the 2016 Euros!

⭐ Ronaldo's iconic goal celebration, 'siu', is actually Portuguese for 'yes'!

STATS:

BORN: 05/02/1985

AGE: 39

POSITION: FORWARD

CLUBS: SPORTING CP, MAN UTD, REAL MADRID, JUVENTUS, MAN UTD, AL NASSR

CLUB APPEARANCES: 1033

GOALS: 776

NATIONAL TEAM: PORTUGAL

INT CAPS: 215

INT GOALS: 135

RONALDO

BY NUMBERS!

We've crunched the stats so that you don't have to!

7

Ronaldo's **iconic shirt number!**

1985 The year Ronaldo was born!

Cristiano's played for five different clubs! **5**

183 Ronaldo's record-breaking number of Champions League appearances!

215 International caps for Portugal, making him the most capped player of all time!

Total number of career goals in official matches! **911**

33

■ Career trophies!

2003

■ The year he first signed for Manchester United (before a short return in 2021)!

■ European Golden Boots won!

4

647,000,000

■ Ronaldo's Instagram followers!

1248+

■ Number of official match appearances – the most for an outfield player EVER!

■ The winning score in the Euro 2016 final (Portugal vs France)

1-0

450

■ Goals scored for Real Madrid – a club record!

€100,000,000

■ Ronaldo's transfer fee going from Real Madrid to Juventus - the most expensive transfer for an Italian club... EVER!

SUPERSTARS VERSUS LEGENDS
YOU DECIDE!

Who would you rather have in your team from these match-ups? Now's your chance to put your football knowledge to the test and compile your ultimate squad!

BECKER vs. BUFFON

WINNER:
SUPERSTAR ☐ LEGEND ☐

OBLAK vs. ČECH

WINNER:
SUPERSTAR ☑ LEGEND ☑

ALEXANDER-ARNOLD vs. CAFU

WINNER:
SUPERSTAR ☑ LEGEND ☑

HERNÁNDEZ vs. EVRA

WINNER:
SUPERSTAR ☑ LEGEND ☑

VAN DIJK vs. STAM

WINNER:
SUPERSTAR ☑ LEGEND ☑

RÜDIGER vs. MALDINI

WINNER:
SUPERSTAR ☑ LEGEND ☑

SALIBA vs. FERDINAND

WINNER:
SUPERSTAR ☑ LEGEND ☑

YAMAL vs. FIGO

WINNER:

SUPERSTAR ☑ LEGEND ☑

GREALISH vs. BALE

WINNER:

SUPERSTAR ☑ LEGEND ☑

GAVI vs. TOURÉ

WINNER:

SUPERSTAR ☑ LEGEND ☑

BELLINGHAM vs. ZIDANE

WINNER:

SUPERSTAR ☑ LEGEND ☑

MAINOO vs. KEANE

WINNER:

SUPERSTAR ☑ LEGEND ☑

HAALAND vs. IBRAHIMOVIĆ

WINNER:

SUPERSTAR ☑ LEGEND ☑

MBAPPÉ vs. HENRY

WINNER:

SUPERSTAR ☑ LEGEND ☑

VINÍCIUS vs. RONALDO

WINNER:

SUPERSTAR ☑ LEGEND ☑

NOW ADD UP ALL YOUR SCORES TO SEE WHAT YOUR TEAM IS MADE OF!

HAVE YOU PACKED IT FULL OF CURRENT SUPERSTARS OR FAVOURED LEGENDS OF THE GAME?

....

POWER PROFILE!

VINICIUS JUNIOR

DAMAGE ALERT!

Even though he's fast and agile, it can sometimes be a struggle for him when faced with tight marking and physical defenders to make his usual impact in a match!

POWER UP!

It's no secret that Vini is excellent at dribbling, but he's also a versatile player. While he mainly plays as a left winger, he's shown that he's more than capable of playing on both wings!

DID YOU KNOW?

⭐ As a child he started out playing futsal and he says this is one of the reasons why he is so skilled at dribbling!

⭐ Football isn't the only sport Vini is interested in, he's also a massive basketball fan!

⭐ He started The Vini Jr. Institute, which gives disadvantaged children in Brazil the chance to get an education and learn new skills, including football!

⭐ He looks up to Neymar and he got the chance to play alongside his football idol when joining the Brazilian national team – that sounds like a dream come true!

STATS:

BORN: 12/07/2000
AGE: 24
POSITION: LEFT WINGER
CLUBS: FLAMENGO, REAL MADRID
CLUB APPEARANCES: 287
GOALS: 97
NATIONAL TEAM: BRAZIL
INT CAPS: 37
INT GOALS: 5

Pics: Shutterstock. (2) Stats correct at time of print.

DESIGN A
TEAM
BADGE
Every football team needs a badge! Create one for your very own dream team!
WHAT'S YOUR TEAM'S NAME?
FC BAYERN MUNCHEN EV
MANCHESTER UNITED FOOTBALL CLUB
PARIS SAINT-GERMAIN 1970
CHELSEA FOOTBALL CLUB
MANCHESTER CITY 18 94
WHEN YOU'VE FINISHED YOUR DRAWING, DON'T FORGET TO ADD A SPLASH OF COLOUR!
WHICH LEAGUE DO THEY PLAY IN?
PREMIER LEAGUE
BUNDESLIGA
LA LIGA
OTHER
Pics: Shutterstock (4)

ROBLOX SOCCER STARS

■ These football games are top of the Blox!

TOUCH FOOTBALL

Whether you just want a fun kickabout with mates, or if you want to go for gold in the Elite Clan League, there's plenty of footy fun to be had in Touch Football! The controls might be simple to learn, but they're hard to master so you'll need to get training if you wanna be a pro!

DID YOU KNOW?

The more wins you have, the higher the rank you can play at!

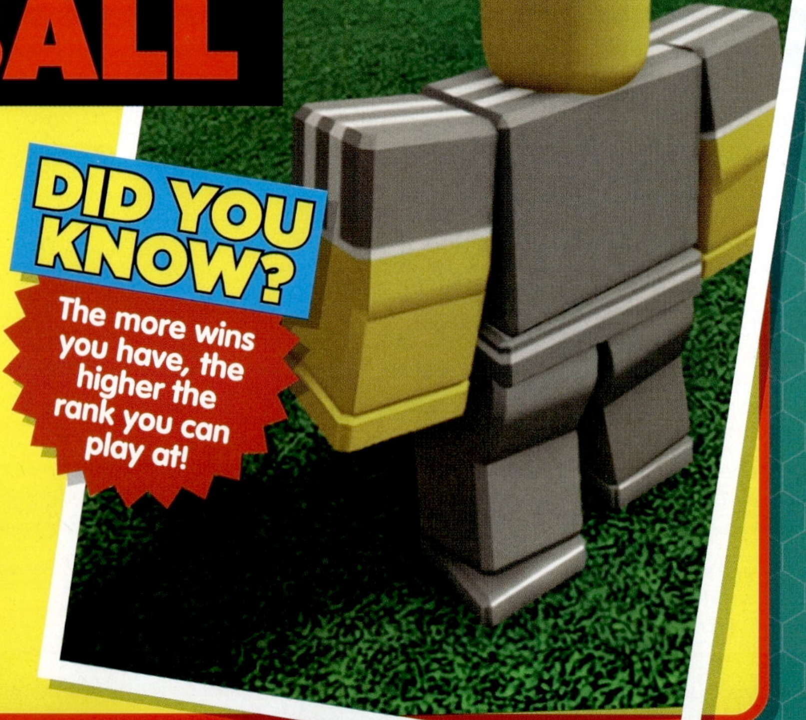

TPS: STREET SOCCER

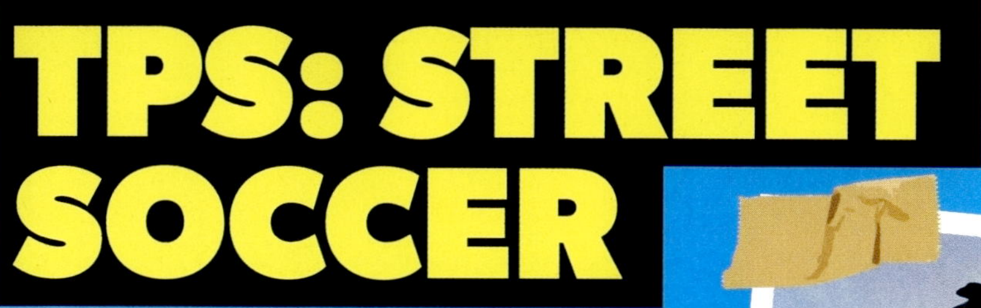

⚽ Show off your soccer skills in style but watch out – this is no ordinary game of football! With knockouts, power shots and even superpowers, **TPS: Street Soccer** will put your tekkers to the test like never before.

SUPER STRIKER LEAGUE

⚽ It's time to take football to the extreme! In **Super Striker League**, there are epic items to unlock and upgrade, power-ups to master, and special abilities to show off, meaning there's never a dull moment – GOOOAAALLL!

WHICH ROBLOX FOOTY GAME IS YOUR FAVE?

....

ROCKET LEAGUE

Everything you need to know about this epic game!

POWER UP YOUR ENGINES

The aim of the game is simple – score goals with giant footballs with rocket-powered cars! Starting on the opposite end of the field from the opposing team, you'll race down the pitch to be the first to the ball. Like regular football, the team with the most goals win.

DID YOU KNOW?

In its first month alone, Rocket League was downloaded over 6 million times!

TOP TIP!

Instead of ball chasing, prioritise smart positioning. This will make the gameplay feel less chaotic and it gives your defence less pressure!

COOL CUSTOMISATION

You'll choose your vehicle before each game and there are loads of customisation options. Stand out and give your car a unique look with various decals, boosts, antennas and more!

AWESOME ESPORTS

Teams from all over the world set their sights on becoming World Champions in the Rocket League Championship Series every year! To get to this stage, teams must prove themselves through qualifiers, tournaments and regular seasons in their local regions.

SUPER SEASONS

Each new season keeps Rocket League fresh and engaging with bug fixes, major content updates and new cosmetics. Whether you're a competitive or casual player, there's something for everyone!

Add some colour to this sweet ride!

POWER PROFILE!

LIONEL MESSI

POWER UP!

Widely regarded one of the greatest of all time, Messi has won a whopping eight Ballon d'Or awards, as well as being crowned World's Best Player by FIFA eight times, too!

DAMAGE ALERT!

Despite being one of the best players in the world, Messi doesn't have the strongest defensive game and struggles in the air. No headers for Lionel!

DID YOU KNOW?

★ Although he was born in Argentina, Messi holds dual citizenship so could have played national football for Spain!

★ He's an Olympic gold medallist after competing for Argentina in the 2008 Beijing Olympic Games!

★ Leo's exceptional agility is often credited to his short height, earning him the nickname 'The Atomic Flea'!

★ In addition to winning many club trophies, Messi picked up one of the biggest prizes of them all when he helped lead Argentina to victory at the 2022 World Cup!

STATS:

BORN: 24/06/1987
AGE: 37
POSITION: FORWARD
CLUBS: BARCELONA, PSG, INTER MIAMI
CLUB APPEARANCES: 914
GOALS: 744
NATIONAL TEAM: ARGENTINA
INT CAPS: 191
INT GOALS: 122

Pics: Shutterstock (1) Stats correct at time of print

MESSI
MASTERCLASS
DON'T BE MESSY, PLAY LIKE MESSI!
LIONEL MESSI IS ONE OF THE ALL-TIME GOATS! HERE'S A STEP-BY-STEP GUIDE THAT'LL HELP YOU LEAVE YOUR OPPONENT IN THE DUST NEXT TIME YOU'RE HAVING A KICKABOUT – MESSI STYLE!
WHEN BEING CLOSELY MARKED BY YOUR OPPONENT, THE AIM IS TO TURN AND BEAT THEM ON THE INSIDE:
1
When the pass is played to you, move towards it.
2
Control the ball when you are facing away from your opponent

3
Glance over your shoulder to see where the defender is before turning.
4
Now facing your opponent, pretend you're going right to trick the defender…
5
…before quickly changing pace and direction and playing the ball with the outside of your left foot.
6
Accelerate past the defender while they are off balance!
REMEMBER IT TAKES PRACTICE - SPEND TIME WITH THE BALL EVERY DAY WEAVING IN AND OUT OF CONES OR IMAGINARY DEFENDERS AND DON'T GIVE UP! GOOD LUCK!

A BEGINNER'S GUIDE TO... FOOTBALL MANAGER

■ Are you new to the legendary Football Manager game? Well, everyone has to start sometime, right? We've got you covered here with tips to keep in mind and give you the best chance of success...

CHOOSE CAREFULLY

First things first, you'll have to decide on what team you want to manage. You could take a team from the lower leagues all the way to the top. However, beware — this will be difficult as you'll have a smaller budget and will need to have a strong eye for a bargain.

Or you could jump straight into managing a top team like Real Madrid or Liverpool with better players, scouting and a bigger transfer budget. Patience may be in shorter supply here, though, and if you get off to a bad start you could find yourself quickly out of a job!

STICK TO WHAT YOU KNOW

There are so many leagues from around the world that you can decide to manage in. However, what do you know about the Japanese J1 League or the Superliga in Denmark? If your knowledge of players and teams in these leagues isn't great, it's going to make your job of getting results more difficult.

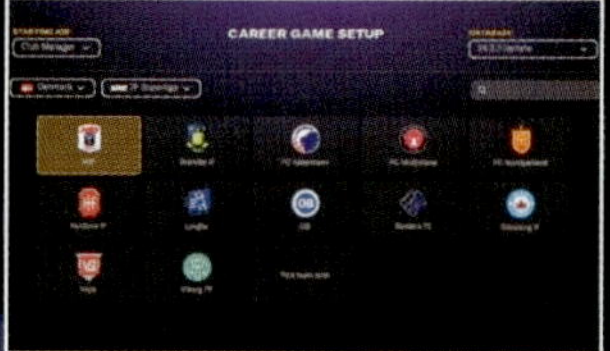

CHOOSE YOUR STYLE

After you've chosen your team, you'll have to decide on what your coaching style is. Coaching styles available are default, disciplinary, motivator, youth development, knowledgeable, tactician, and taskmaster. Do you want to be a tactician like Pep or a Diego Simeone-type with a strong disciplined approach?

IT'S A TEAM GAME

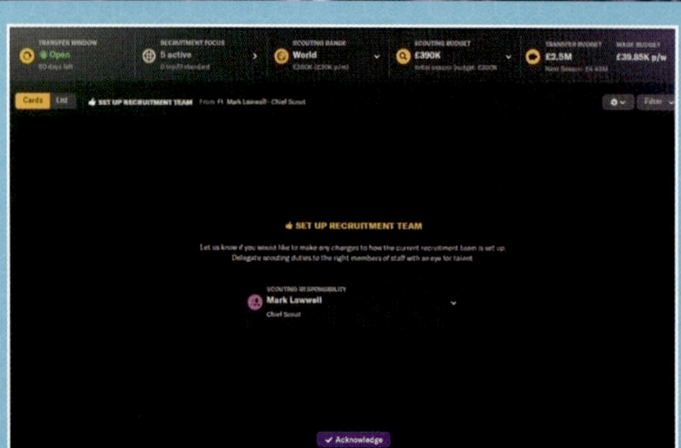

You'll want to be the main person managing your team, of course, but there's plenty more to it, and that's where your staff can help! From assistant coaches to scouts, use them wisely. We recommend spending time at the outset organising your staff, delegating some tasks to them and making sure you aren't left to do everything.

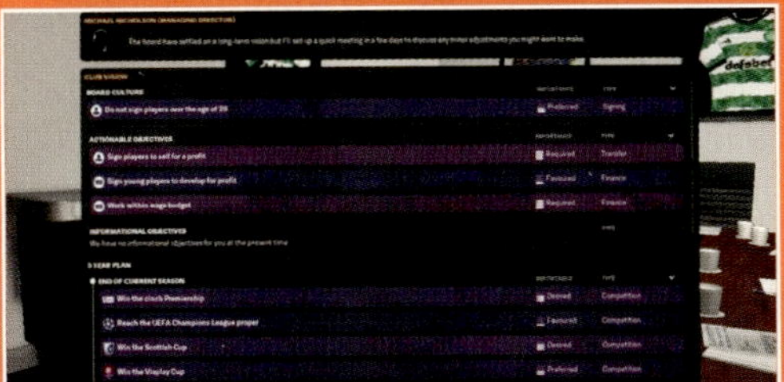

Signing for a club and winning matches may not be enough to keep your job. You must match the club's vision or else your contract will be terminated. If the club wants to win trophies or finish in a certain league position and you agree with their vision, then it's up to you to deliver.

MANAGE YOUR PLAYERS' MORALE

If you have poor team morale it can lead to a run of poor results that's hard to stop. Unhappiness in the camp can also lead to players making demands to play in a certain position or requesting a transfer away from the club. The key here is to pick your moments when criticising your team and not shout at them every week! On the flipside be sure to praise players by talking to them individually when they've had a good game or trained well.

TACTICAL PLAN

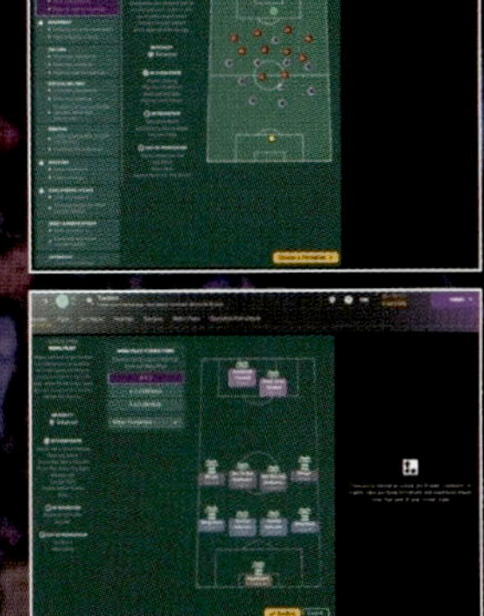

There are so many possibilities when it comes to tactics and formations. You can keep things simple or complicated. An important thing to consider is, do you have the right players to play in your preferred system? For example, why play with wing-backs if you don't have good wing-backs in your squad?

Consider also a plan B formation. It may not be best to set up against an elite European opponent the same way you did the week before against lower league opposition. Having a plan B tactic also allows you to change things in game if plan A isn't working.

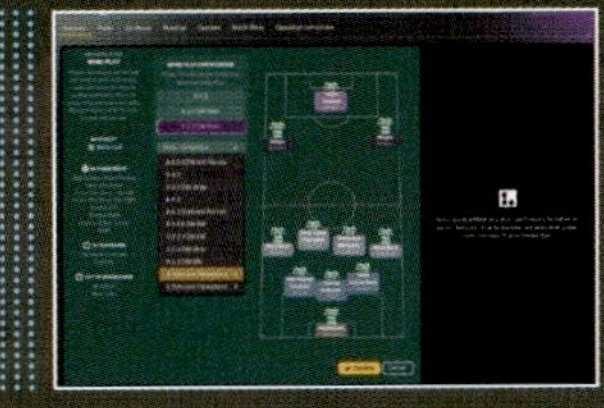

USE SCOUTS EFFECTIVELY

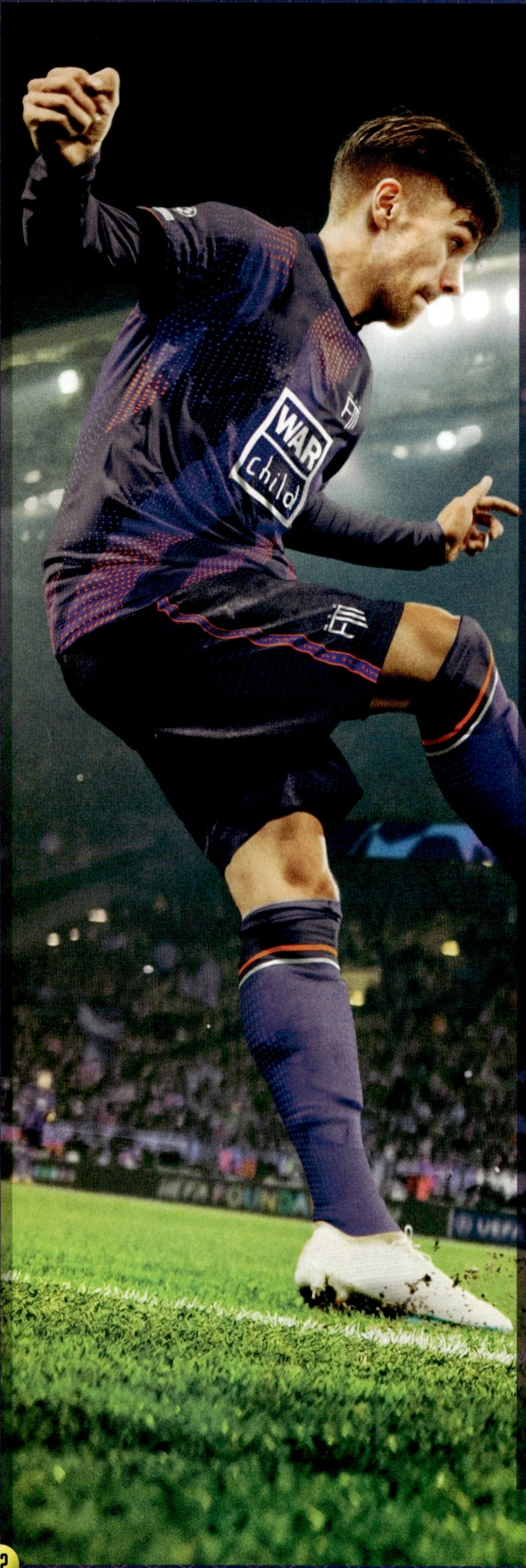

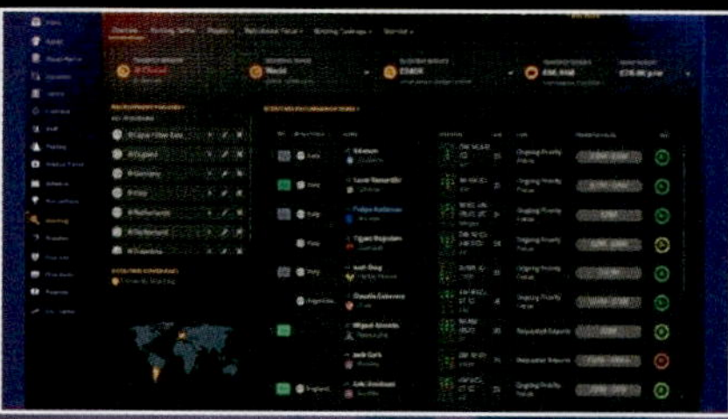

If you want to get the best value for money and spot players your opponents may have missed, then it's important to make good use of your scouts. Assigning them to regions or leagues where there are untapped markets, such as South America, Eastern Europe or Africa, can sometimes produce hidden gems.

SEARCH FOR WHAT YOU NEED

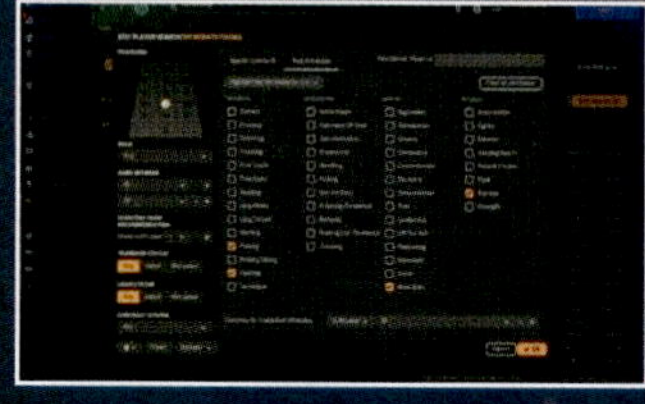

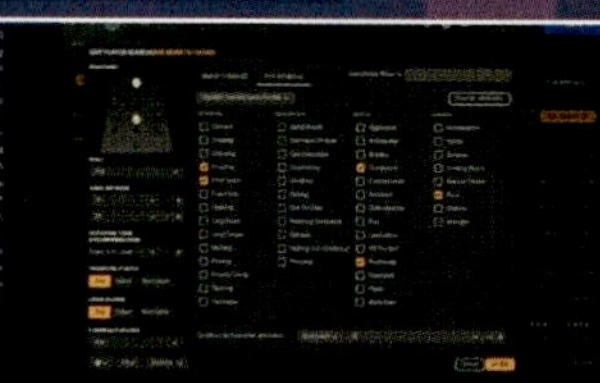

In **FM** you can quickly search for specific types of players by highlighting their key attributes. For example, if it's a box-to-box midfielder you need, then prioritise physical traits like stamina and work-rate alongside technical ones like passing and tackling. If it's a goal scorer you're after, you'll want to prioritise finishing, first touch, composure, positioning and pace.

KEEP ON TOP OF YOUR INBOX

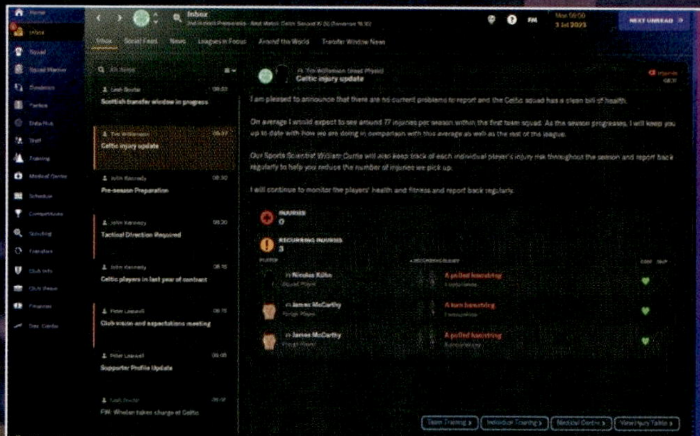

Your inbox will always be filled with messages, and it helps to keep up-to-date with it. You can access and act on a whole range of topics such as scouting reports, injury updates, training results, board comms and transfer negotiations.

TRANSFER NEGOTIATIONS

Once you've spotted the player you want to sign, the tough part begins. Agreeing a fee with the club may not be straightforward and even if you get past that part successfully, there's then the question of whether the player is interested in moving to your club. If they are, there's the further challenge of agreeing contract length, weekly wage and any clauses within.

Before making a bid for any player you should contact their agent to find out if they're available and interested.

When submitting a bid, consider paying in instalments over a number of seasons. For example, you can split the fee over three instalments over 12 months. You can even make the bid more attractive by adding clauses such as an extra fee after X amount of league appearances. Steps such as this can ensure you don't blow all your transfer budget on one player.

When negotiating the contract, a player may ask for guarantees that they'll be played in a specific position. Think carefully before agreeing to this. Simply agreeing to get the transfer over the line and then not honouring that agreement will only lead to the player getting unhappy and potentially requesting a transfer.

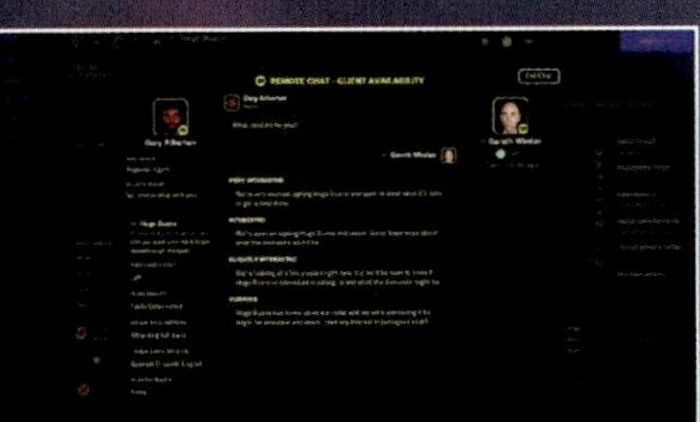

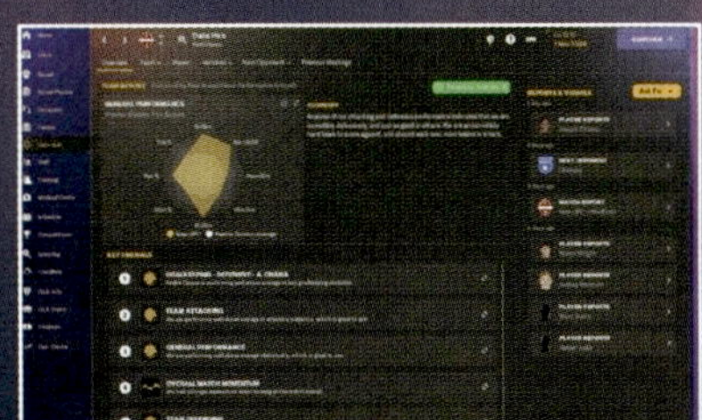

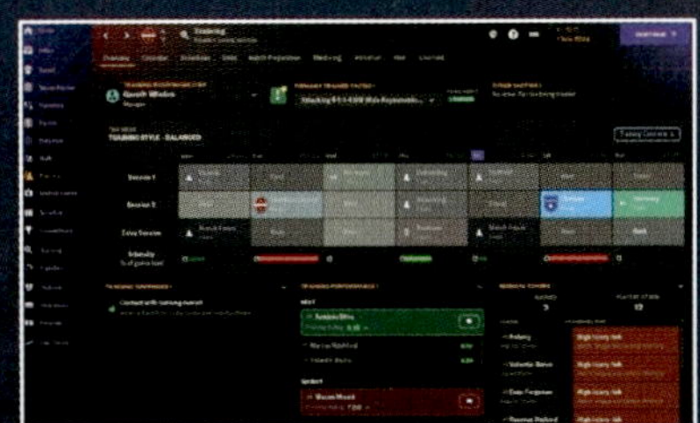

TAKE YOUR TIME

Finally, there's so much to being a manager on **Football Manager**. Just like in real-life, there are so many things to consider on top of simply playing a football match. You might switch it on, play for an hour or two and only manage to play one or two fixtures. That's okay if that happens, there's no need to rush through a season. Play too quickly and you're more likely to make tactical errors or miss out on a wonderkid signing!

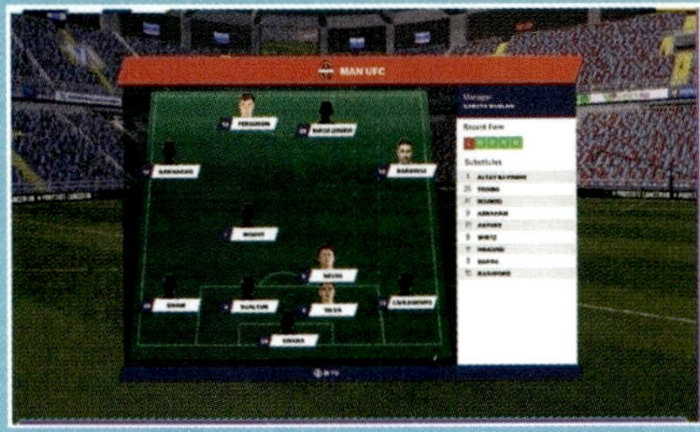

MINECRAFT SUPER STADIUM

GO FOR GOLD WITH YOUR VERY OWN SPORTS ARENA!

SOCCER SKILLS!

Build yourself a football pitch, complete with white wool goalposts and cobweb nets. You can even bring your pitch to life with our Woof Ball tutorial below!

AWESOME ATHLETICS!

Run circles around your mates by building an awesome racetrack around your stadium. Add in some fences for hurdles to really show off your sporty skills!

WOOF BALL!

MAKE YOUR OWN SOCCER-STYLE MINIGAME WITHOUT ANY MODS!

1 Build your pitch out of packed ice blocks and cover with green and white carpet to get that classic football look, but with added slide!

SUPER SCORES!

No stadium would be complete without a giant scoreboard! Use wool for a pixel art creation, or if you're up for the challenge, you can even make moving elements with redstone.

TOP TEAMS!

Create dugouts or seating areas for each team and then decorate them in your fave colours. Don't forget to include a tunnel that takes you to each team's locker room… or a secret base hidden under your stadium!

2 Tame a **Wolf** and make them sit – this is your ball!

3 Thanks to the slippery ice, when you run into a sitting **Wolf**, it'll slide across the pitch, just like a football! GOOOAAALLL!

eSports: A PRO GUIDE!

PLAY WITH PALS!

Even if you hope to one day be competing against them, playing with your friends is a great way for you to improve as a player. You can help each other improve, share tactics and it just makes practising so much more fun!

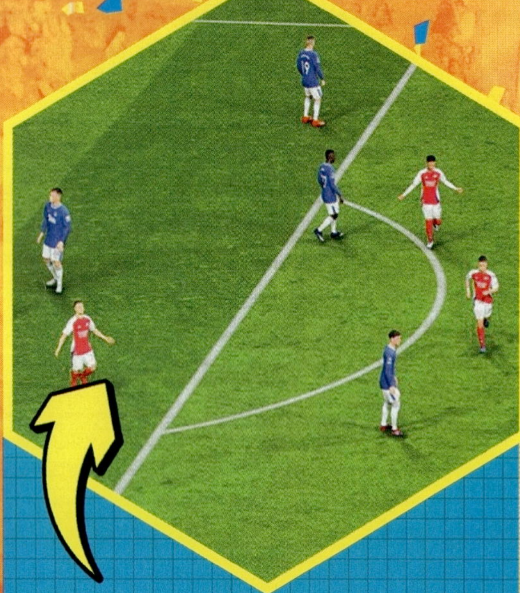

POSITION PRO!

Football is all about teamwork! It's important to understand what each position does and how different formations work. Knowing when to attack or defend can make a big difference!

HIT RECORD!

Every modern console and most top eSports games have a way of recording your gameplay to watch back later. Use it! Watching yourself play lets you work out what you do well and what you've still got to improve on.

SUPER STREAMER!

Ever wonder why pro gamers stream all the time too? Loads of pros feel like having an audience helps them to always play their best as it's much harder to be lazy or slack off when you've got someone watching your every move!

WATCH THE BEST!

Pro gamers don't live in a bubble. Being good at a game isn't enough, you need to be able to anticipate how your opponents will play and be able to counter it. Watching the top players will give you an idea of what to be ready to play against.

BOSS BALANCE!

The top-tier of pros have personal coaches to make sure they eat right, sleep right and prevent work or school from distracting them from their gaming goals. You don't need a coach, but you do need to keep a healthy gaming/life balance.

LASER FOCUS!

No-one is the master of every game. Professional players stick to one game, so they know it inside and out. This allows them to learn the right strategies and tricks to give them an edge over their opponents and train smarter. In eSports, it's all about picking one thing to be the best at!

eSports FOOTBALL CHAMPS!

MANCHESTER UNITED

■ Man Utd haven't just been battling it out in the 24/25 ePremier League, with players showing off their **EAS FC** skills, but the Red Devils have also teamed up with **Konami** to host their own eFootball 2025 Club Event!

MANCHESTER CITY

■ One of the most successful teams in recent history, City have won the PL EIGHT times since the 2011/2012 season! But their success doesn't stop there – pro **EAS FC** players **Tekkz** and **Bonanno** led the club to their second ePremier League trophy when they scooped the title in 2024!

WHY ESPORTS?!

■ It might seem random for your fave footy club to have an eSports division, but here's a few good reasons why!

1 It helps the club to engage with a different audience, potentially drawing in a new generation of fans!

FC SCHALKE 04

🟨 German side Schalke were one of the first footy teams to jump into the world of eSports back in 2016! They didn't start with a football game though, instead getting players to play **League of Legends**! The club have since gone on to compete in **FIFAe** and Virtual Bundesliga tournaments!

PARIS SAINT-GERMAIN

🟥 Big spenders PSG are a force in eSports as well as footy IRL! In addition to having their own eSports studio and academy, their **EAS FC** team have scooped six major titles, winning big at events like the Esports World Convention. They also have teams that compete in **Rocket League** and **Brawl Stars**, too!

FC BARCELONA

🟥 Not only are FC Barcelona official partners with **eFootball** creators, **Konami**, but they also have a whole bunch of professional eSports teams who have bossed games like **League of Legends**, **Rocket League**, and of course, **eFootball**!

2 New sponsors, advertising, brand partnerships, and creating merchandise for their eSports teams, are all ways for clubs to grow and make more money!

3 eSports events allow clubs to develop new sponsorships and partnerships that they might not have otherwise.

GOAL GETTER!

Make the right decisions to take your team to the top!

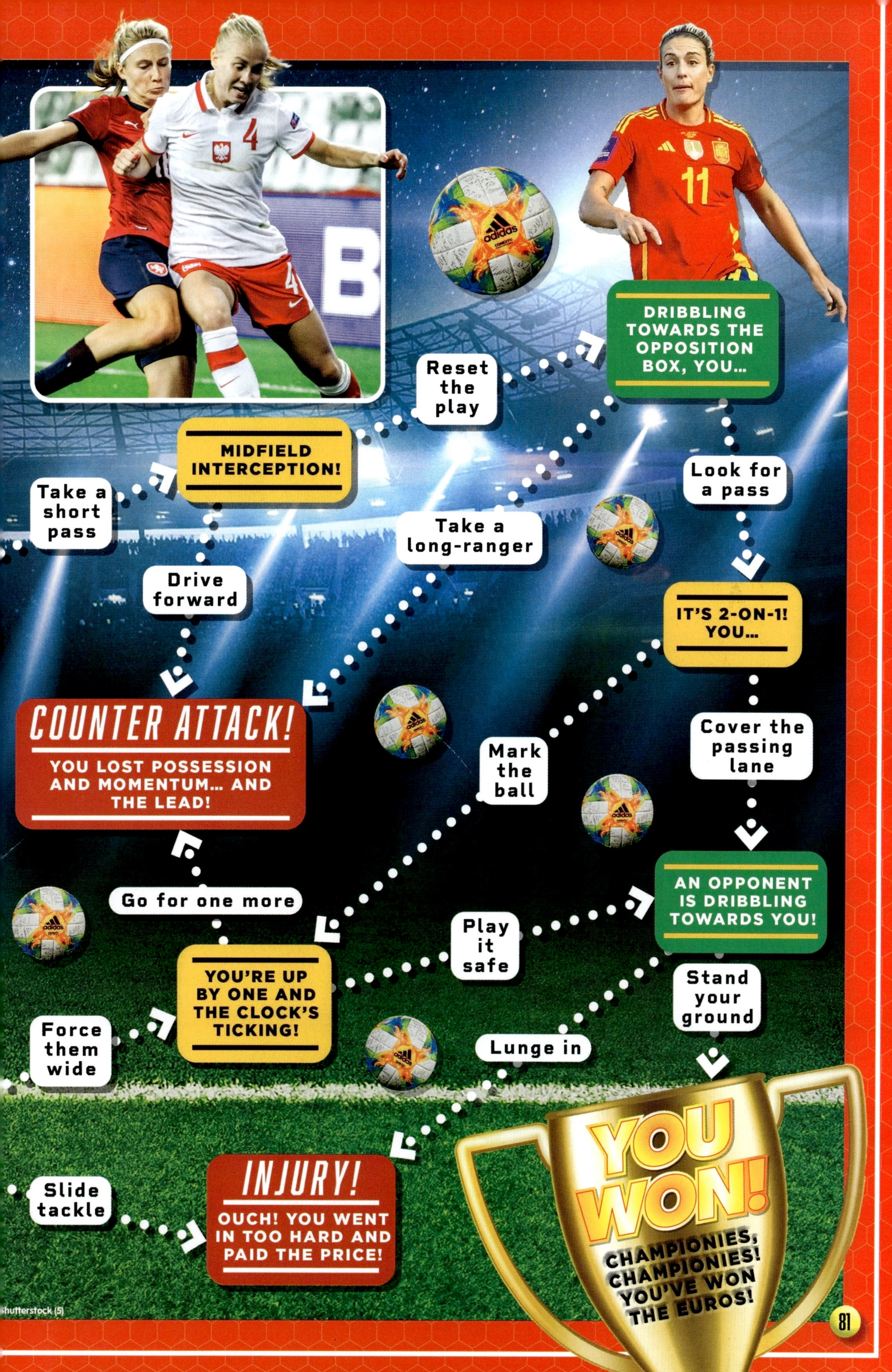

Reset the play
MIDFIELD INTERCEPTION!
DRIBBLING TOWARDS THE OPPOSITION BOX, YOU...
Look for a pass
Take a short pass
Take a long-ranger
Drive forward
IT'S 2-ON-1! YOU...
COUNTER ATTACK!
YOU LOST POSSESSION AND MOMENTUM... AND THE LEAD!
Mark the ball
Cover the passing lane
Go for one more
Play it safe
AN OPPONENT IS DRIBBLING TOWARDS YOU!
YOU'RE UP BY ONE AND THE CLOCK'S TICKING!
Force them wide
Lunge in
Stand your ground
Slide tackle
INJURY!
OUCH! YOU WENT IN TOO HARD AND PAID THE PRICE!
YOU WON!
CHAMPIONIES, CHAMPIONIES! YOU'VE WON THE EUROS!

Brush up on your footy facts!

STRANGE BUT TRUE!

1
Keeper Tom King broke the world record when he scored from 96.01m! That's the same height as Big Ben!

2
Italy won the 1968 European Championship semi-final... by a coin toss!

3
In 2011, a record 36 red cards were dished out during a match in Argentina!

4
AC Milan and Inter Milan were originally one club who split up after a disagreement!

5
A Dutch referee accidentally scored a goal in a third division match – and it counted!

POR FAVOR DEJA!

82

6

7

8

9

10

11

12

13

14

15

16

17

18

Shutterstock (8)

*Facts and figures correct at time of print

THEY COST HOW MUCH?!

TOP 5 MOST EXPENSIVE!

1. **NEYMAR** – BARCELONA TO PSG – 2017 – £200 MILLION (APPROX.)

2. **KYLIAN MBAPPÉ** – AS MONACO TO PSG – 2017 – £166 MILLION

3. **PHILIPPE COUTINHO** – LIVERPOOL TO BARCELONA – 2018 – £146 MILLION

4. **JOÃO FÉLIX** – BENFICA TO ATLÉTICO MADRID – 2019 – £113 MILLION

5. **ANTOINE GRIEZMANN** – ATLÉTICO MADRID TO BARCELONA – 2019 – £107 MILLION

WHAT A WASTE OF MONEY!

While Real Madrid usually get it right, they'll certainly rue spending nearly £89 million on **Eden Hazard** in 2019. The transfer fee plus a reported £400,000 a week in wages ended up a disastrous piece of business. **Hazard** scored only one goal in the 2019/2020 season and ended his career there playing just 76 games in four seasons, scoring only seven goals.

£100,000 TRANSFER
■ **Denis Law** became the first British player to be sold for £100,000 in 1961 when he joined Torino from Manchester City.

£1,000,000 TRANSFER
■ In 1979, **Trevor Francis** became the first British footballer to command a £1 million transfer fee when he made the move from Birmingham City to Nottingham Forest.

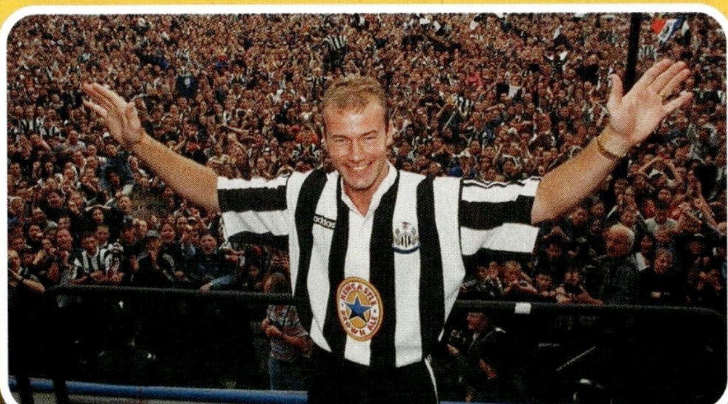

£10,000,000 TRANSFER
■ The first footballer to cost more than £10 million in a transfer fee was **Alan Shearer** in 1996, when he signed for Newcastle United from Blackburn Rovers for £15 million. This made him the most expensive footballer in history at the time.

£100,000,000 TRANSFER
■ The first footballer to cost more than £100 million in transfer fee was **Neymar's** move from Barcelona to PSG. This isn't just the most expensive in history, it was also the first to happen costing more than £100 million in transfer fees.

FREE AND EASY!

Spending money ought to give a greater chance of success, but sometimes the best things in ~~life~~ football are free! Here are two examples of when a free transfer proved to be great value!

SOL CAMPBELL
■ He once did the unthinkable in 2001 and left Tottenham on a free transfer to sign for North London rivals Arsenal. The risk paid off as he went on to win two Premier League titles with the Gunners, including the 2003/04 Invincibles season.

ANDREA PIRLO
■ He was already an Italy and AC Milan legend and considered one of the world's best midfielders in 2011. He then surprised everyone by leaving Milan and signing for rivals Juventus on a free transfer. Fans couldn't believe their luck as he went on to spend four seasons there, winning four league titles in the process.

SEEING RED!

WHERE DID IT ALL BEGIN?

Before 1970 players used to be sent off via a verbal warning from a referee. However, without cards, it was hard for any viewer at home or in the stadium to know what was going on. So, yellow and red cards were introduced at the FIFA World Cup in 1970 with the first red card in a major tournament shown four years later at the next World Cup in West Germany.

VAMOS RAMOS

Real Madrid and Spain icon Sergio Ramos has certainly enjoyed a storied career filled with prestigious trophies, but he has also made headlines for his fondness for receiving red cards. Remarkably, he's been shown the red card 29 times throughout his career!

BLUE FOLLOWED BY RED

Everton, with 108 red cards have the most of any team since the Premier League was formed in 1992. However, Arsenal follow close behind on 107.*

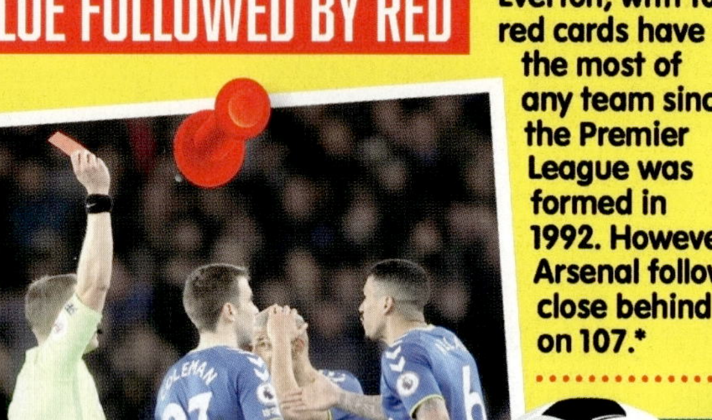

THE HEADBUTT

Zinedine Zidane was the star captain of France in the 2006 World Cup, winning the Golden Ball as the tournament's best player. In a dramatic final, he shocked everyone by headbutting Italian player Marco Materazzi, earning one of the most infamous red cards of all. France lost to Italy on penalties, and Zidane's final match was marked by that unforgettable moment.

RECORD BREAKER

Retired Columbian player, Gerardo Bedoya, holds the record for being sent off a wild 46 times! Known as 'The Beast' for his tough tackles, he was once suspended for 15 matches. After retiring, he briefly tried coaching but was dismissed after just 21 minutes!

WHY RED MATTERS

Looking at every fixture from the Premier League a few seasons back, 59% of teams who received a red card went on to lose the match. 18% of the time they managed a draw, and they only won 23% of the time – less than one in four.

* Stats correct at time of going to press.

POWER PROFILE!

AITANA BONMATÍ

POWER UP!

Many consider Aitana to be the best women's football player in the world and it's easy to see why! She's always aware of her surroundings, allowing her to adapt and stay one step ahead of her opponents.

DAMAGE ALERT!

While she's a leader in midfield and has the skills to get into the box, defence is one of her weaker areas. This is because of her lack of physicality and disadvantage in aerial duels.

DID YOU KNOW?

⭐ **Aitana** was part of the first team in the history of Barcelona FC to win the UEFA Women's Champions League!

⭐ She joined Barcelona's youth team at 14-years-old and would travel almost two hours on public transport with her dad to get to training – now that's dedication!

⭐ She won the Women's Ballon d'Or award in 2023 and again in 2024. This is a huge deal because it's one of the most prestigious individual awards in football!

⭐ When she's not playing football, she enjoys travelling and says it's her favourite way to disconnect.

STATS:

BORN: 18/01/1998

AGE: 27

POSITION: MIDFIELDER

CLUBS: BARCELONA

CLUB APPEARANCES: 280

GOALS: 100

NATIONAL TEAM: SPAIN

INT CAPS: 72

INT GOALS: 28

Pics: Shutterstock (1) Stats correct at time of print

BUILD YOUR DREAM FOOTBALL T

CHOOSE YOUR PLAYERS FOR EACH POSITION FROM EACH ROW – REAL FOOTBALLER, OR EPIC GAME CHARACTER? YOU DECIDE!

GOALKEEPERS

PICK 1 KEEPER!

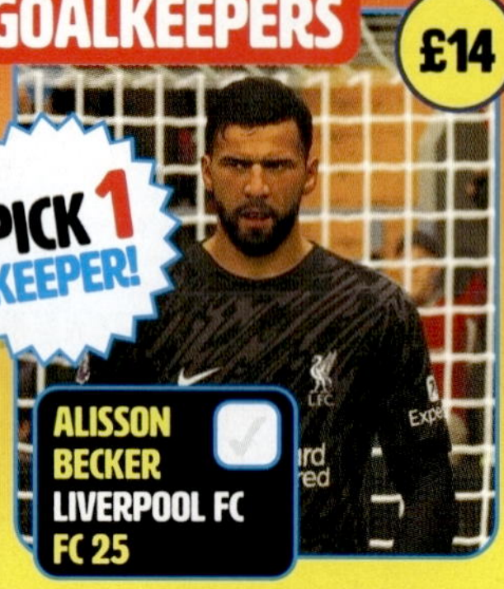

£14

ALISSON BECKER
LIVERPOOL FC
FC 25

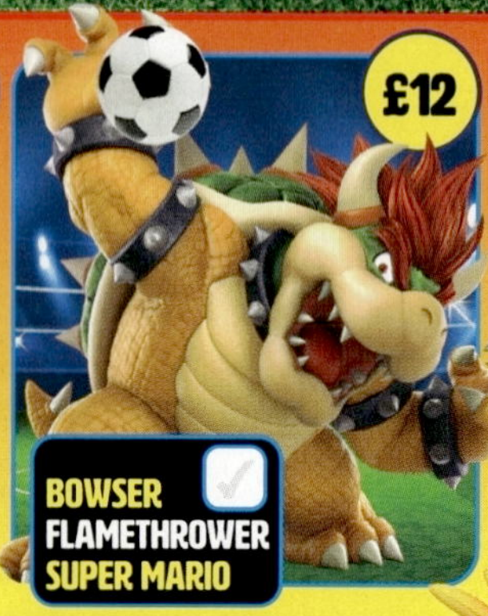

£12

BOWSER
FLAMETHROWER
SUPER MARIO

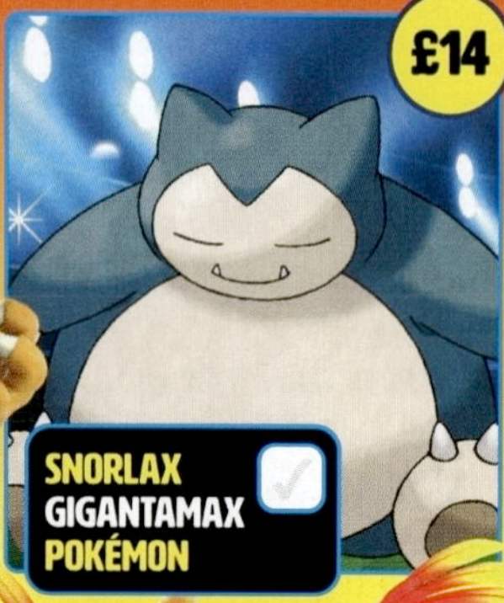

£14

SNORLAX
GIGANTAMAX
POKÉMON

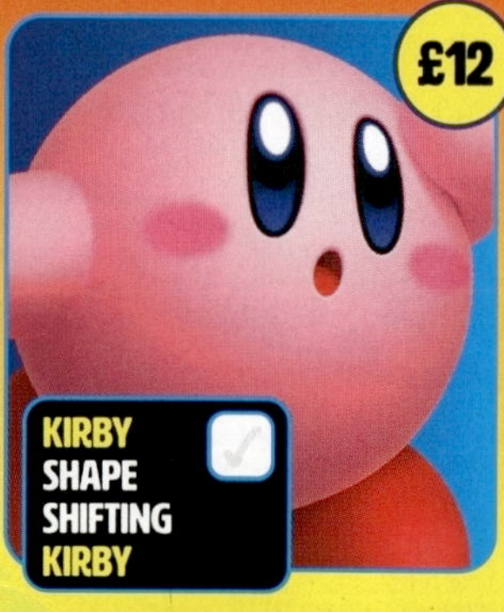

£12

KIRBY
SHAPE SHIFTING
KIRBY

DEFENDERS

PICK 2 DEFENDERS!

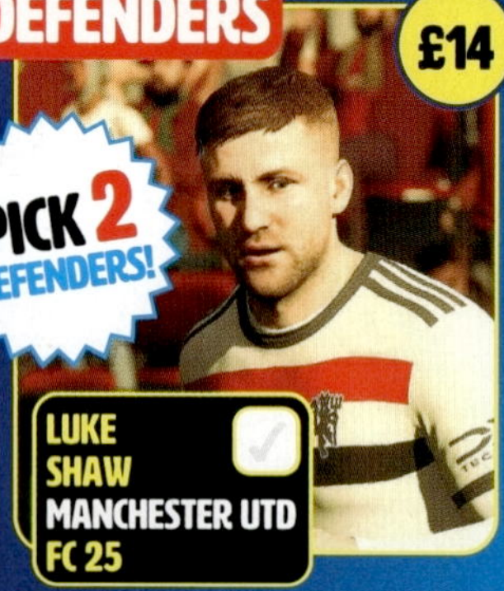

£14

LUKE SHAW
MANCHESTER UTD
FC 25

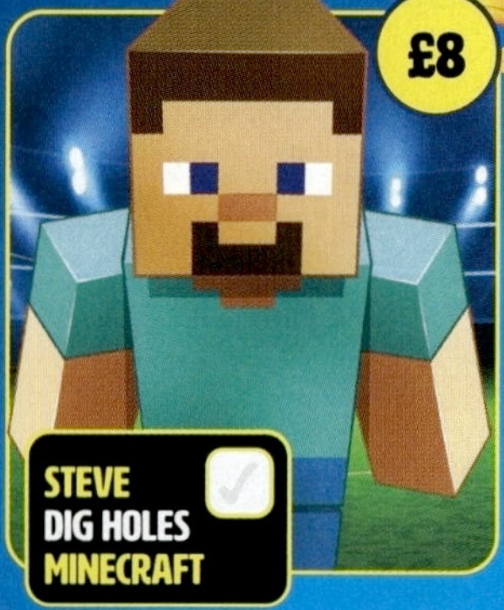

£8

STEVE
DIG HOLES
MINECRAFT

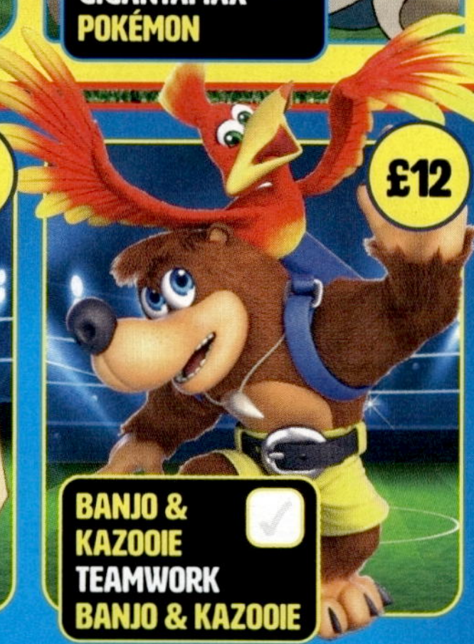

£12

BANJO & KAZOOIE
TEAMWORK
BANJO & KAZOOIE

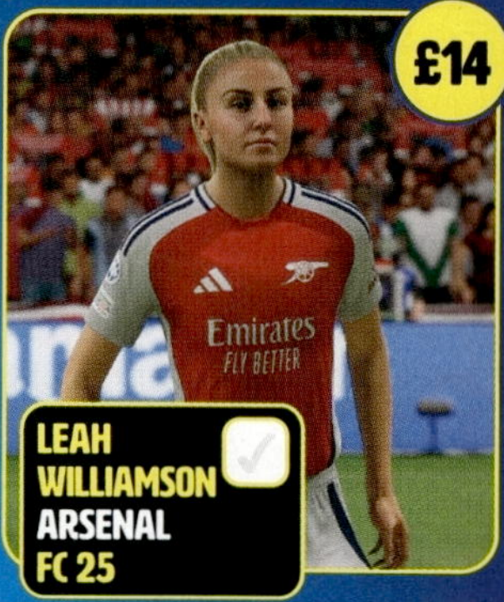

£14

LEAH WILLIAMSON
ARSENAL
FC 25

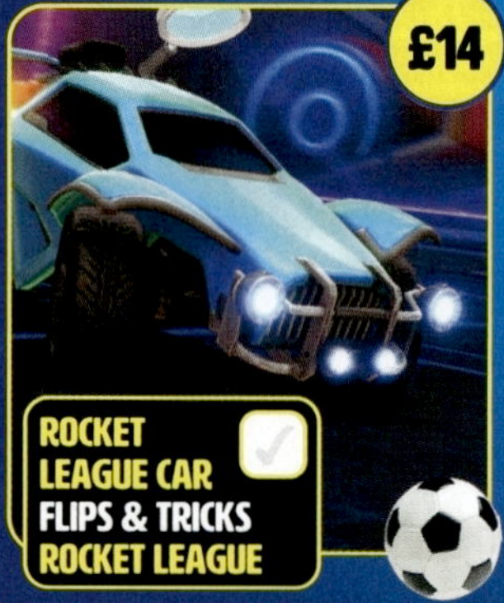

£14

ROCKET LEAGUE CAR
FLIPS & TRICKS
ROCKET LEAGUE

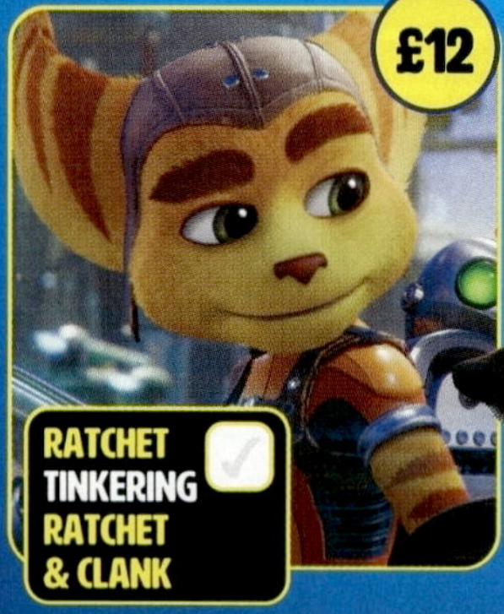

£12

RATCHET
TINKERING
RATCHET & CLANK

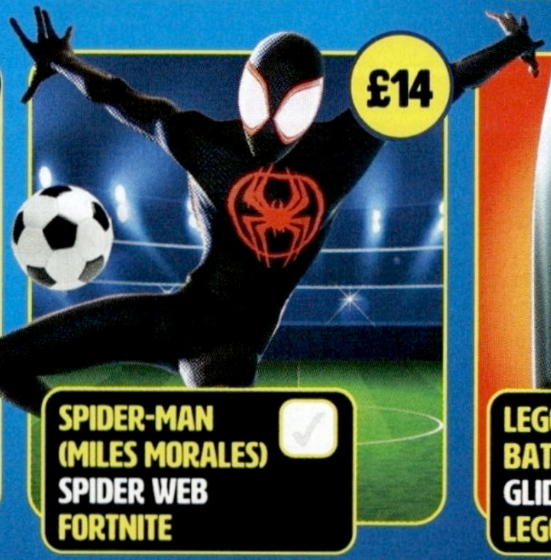

£14

SPIDER-MAN (MILES MORALES)
SPIDER WEB
FORTNITE

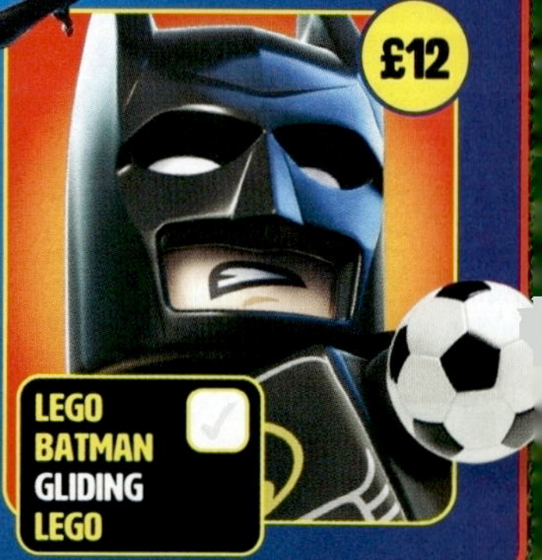

£12

LEGO BATMAN
GLIDING
LEGO

WINGERS

PICK 2 WINGERS!

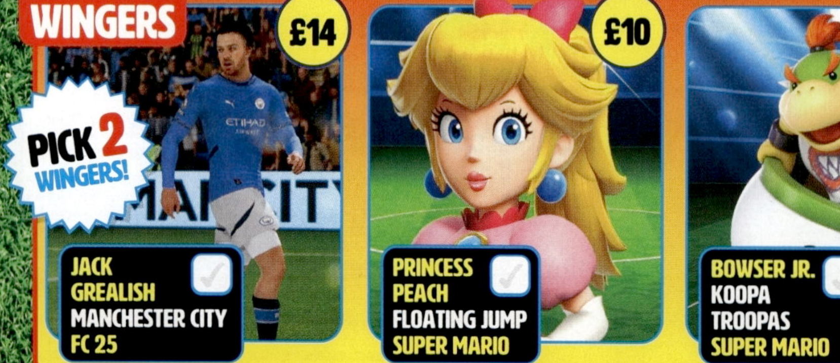

£14

JACK GREALISH
MANCHESTER CITY
FC 25

£10

PRINCESS PEACH
FLOATING JUMP
SUPER MARIO

£8

BOWSER JR.
KOOPA TROOPAS
SUPER MARIO

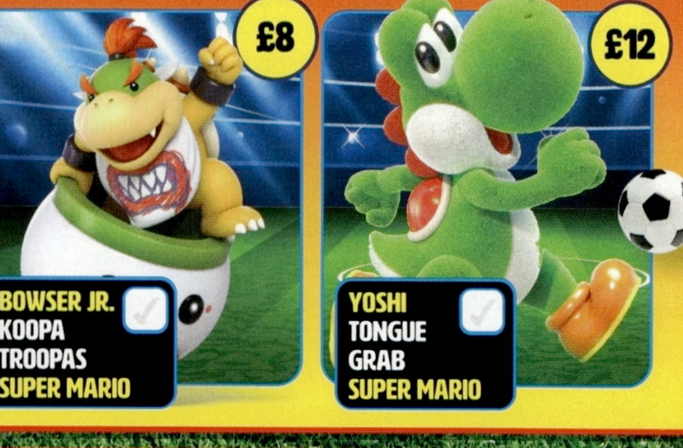

£12

YOSHI
TONGUE GRAB
SUPER MARIO

...EAM

MIDFIELDERS

PICK 4 MIDFIELDERS!

£14

RIVET
DIMENSION
TRAVEL
RATCHET & CLANK

£8

TOM NOOK
BUSINESS
SAVVY
ANIMAL CROSSING

£12

SORA
KEYBLADE
WIELDER
KINGDOM HEARTS

£14

COLE
PALMER
CHELSEA
FC 25

£14

WII FIT
TRAINER
STAMINA
WII FIT

£10

AUDINO
HEALING
POKÉMON

£12

SAMUS
WEAPONS
METROID

£14

JUDE
BELLINGHAM
REAL MADRID
FC 25

STRIKERS

PICK 2 STRIKERS!

£14

ERLING
HAALAND
MANCHESTER CITY
FC 25

£8

AMONG US
CREWMATE
SNEAKY
AMONG US

£10

PIKACHU
ELECTRIC
STRIKE
POKÉMON

£14

LINK
SHIELD
SURF
THE LEGEND OF ZELDA

£14

SONIC
SPEED
SONIC

£14

MAYRA
RAMIREZ
CHELSEA
FC 25

£10

INKLING
PAINT GUN
SPLATOON

£12

MARIO
HAT POWER
SUPER MARIO

TOTAL SPEND = £........

REAL MADRID

Check out all you need to know about the world's most valuable football club.

Real Madrid was founded in 1902 but didn't begin playing in their home stadium, the Santiago Bernabéu, until it was opened in 1947.

In international football, they've won a record 34 trophies which includes a record-breaking 15 European Cup/UEFA Champions League titles.

They're one of three founding members of La Liga that have never been relegated from the top flight, the others being Barcelona and Athletic Bilbao.

Raúl holds the record for most Real Madrid appearances, having played a whopping 741 first-team matches from 1994 to 2010.

Real Madrid's biggest rivalry is with Barcelona with the fixture known as El Clásico which means "The Classic".

They've broken the world transfer fee record four times in their history: In 2000, **Luís Figo** was bought from Barcelona for £54 million, in 2001 **Zinedine Zidane** arrived for £69.75 million, it was **Cristiano Ronaldo** that signed in 2009 for £80 million, while in 2013 **Gareth Bale** cost £85.3 million.

■ Holding over 81,000 people, The Santiago Bernabéu is the third largest stadium in Europe behind the Camp Nou and Wembley. It also had a retractable roof installed in 2023 which retracts in 15 minutes.

As stadium tours go, Real Madrid has one of the best. If you get a chance to visit, you'll see an awesome trophy exhibition, take part in a Walk of Legends, walk pitch side and take your seat in the dugout.

■ **Cristiano Ronaldo** is their all-time top goalscorer with an astounding 450 goals in 438 matches. Contained within the 450 goals are an extraordinary 44 hat-tricks – another Real record!

■ Their record win came way back in 1943 when they defeated arch-rivals Barcelona 11-1!

■ Atlético Madrid are Real Madrid's city rivals, and the teams have faced off in nearly 250 matches over the years. Real have enjoyed more success, winning nearly twice as many matches as their rivals.

■ They are the most valuable football club in the world, worth over £1 billion and topping the 2024 rankings ahead of Manchester City and Barcelona.

DESIGN A FOOTBALL STRIP!

Design a slick new kit for your top football team! Use your favourite colours and patterns to create something unique and eye-catching. You could give a nod to your club's history or create something totally brand new that nobody's ever seen before. Don't forget to include your team's logo!

FUN FACT!

Lionel Messi's jersey was the best-selling football shirt in 2024!

NEED INSPIRATION?

THERE ARE PLENTY OF ICONIC AND COLOURFUL KITS OUT THERE! IF YOU'RE STUCK, WHY NOT USE THESE KITS AS INSPIRATION?

BORUSSIA DORTMUND

GIRONA

WERDER BREMEN

DID YOU KNOW?

The earliest historical record of football clothing is from 1526, when King Henry VIII's Great Wardrobe mentioned football boots!

FOOTBALL'S GREATEST RIVALRIES

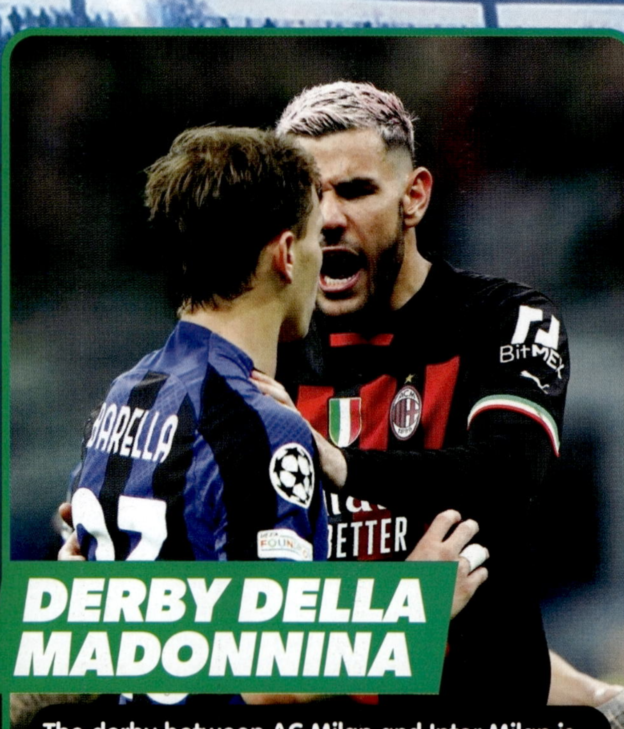

DERBY DELLA MADONNINA

The derby between AC Milan and Inter Milan is another which divides the city. It's made all the more special by the fact both share the famous San Siro stadium, taking turns to be the home team. In terms of matches, Inter shade the rivalry having won more matches, however, AC Milan have the edge when it comes to trophies, including seven European Cups versus Inter's three.

SUPERCLÁSICO

This fierce rivalry takes place between the two most popular and successful clubs in Argentina – Boca Juniors and River Plate. Whether it takes place at Boca's La Bombonera stadium or River's El Monumental, the noise, pyrotechnics, fireworks and iconic kits all lead to an extraordinary sight.

EL CLÁSICO

The match-up between Real Madrid and Barcelona, known as El Clásico, is one of the most iconic rivalries in football. Both sides have huge worldwide fanbases and are often competing for domestic and European trophies every season. The list of players to have played in this fixture over the years reads like a who's who of greatest players, now spearheaded by a new generation of talent such as Vini Jr., Mbappé, Yamal and Pedri.

NORTH WEST DERBY

The match-up between Liverpool and Manchester United may not be a same city rivalry (known as a derby), but it's still massive and one of the most watched games of football worldwide each season. It's a rivalry where each has enjoyed periods of dominance with Liverpool getting the upper hand in recent seasons.

GLASGOW DERBY

The rivalry between Celtic FC and Rangers FC is one of the oldest rivalries in football with their first meeting taking place in 1888. They've gone on to play well over 400 matches against each other and dominate Scottish football in the process, collectively winning over 230 trophies, with Celtic leading the head-to-head in match wins.

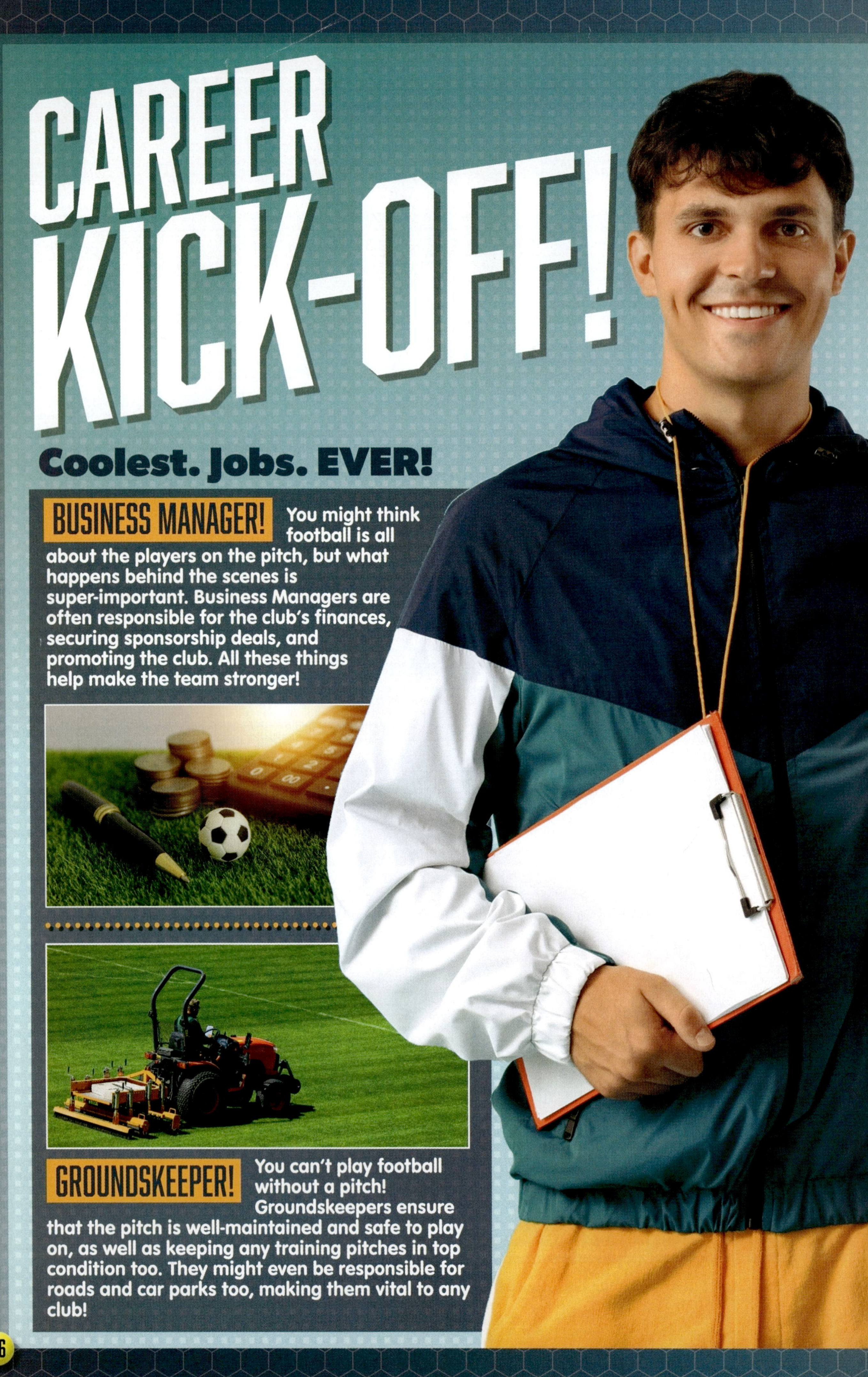

CAREER KICK-OFF!

Coolest. Jobs. EVER!

BUSINESS MANAGER! You might think football is all about the players on the pitch, but what happens behind the scenes is super-important. Business Managers are often responsible for the club's finances, securing sponsorship deals, and promoting the club. All these things help make the team stronger!

GROUNDSKEEPER! You can't play football without a pitch! Groundskeepers ensure that the pitch is well-maintained and safe to play on, as well as keeping any training pitches in top condition too. They might even be responsible for roads and car parks too, making them vital to any club!

COACHING STAFF!

Coaches come up with the team's strategies and training plans, allowing them to play to the best of their ability. Not only will you need to have an elect understanding of the game to be a coach, but you'll also need to be a strong team leader that your players trust!

PHYSIOTHERAPIST!

Football can be tough on even the fittest athlete's body — that's where physiotherapists come in! Not only can they help players rehab injuries and get back to match fitness, but they can also work to prevent injuries and improve player performance, too!

SCOUT!

Fancy watching games for a living? Then scouting might be for you! Scouts are always on the lookout for new talent that can strengthen their club's side. This involves watching games, evaluating potential players and making recommendations to the club.

COMMUNITY MANAGER!

Community Managers help to build the relationship between the club and the town or city they're based in. This might mean organising events to promote the club, managing social media accounts to interact with fans, or even raising money for local charities!

SPORTS MEDIA!

From television to newspapers, radio to social media, there are so many ways to get involved in the media side of football! Commentators, broadcasters, camera operators, photographers, journalists, podcasters, sound technicians... the list of possible media careers goes on – and on!

DID YOU KNOW?

THE AWARD GOES TO…

Lionel Messi! With a total of 41 records to his name, Lionel Messi has been awarded the most Guinness World Records in football.

WHAT A HOOT!

The Finnish football team's mascot, Bubi, was inspired by a real-life eagle owl who flew downs and perched itself on the team's goalpost during their 2008 Euros qualifier match with Belgium. The unfazed owl paused play for 6 minutes!

FOUL BEHAVIOUR!

Keith Gillespie of Sheffield United is the only player to have ever been given a red card before even starting play.

INK-REDIBLE PREDICTIONS!

A German octopus named Paul correctly predicted the outcomes of seven of Germany's World Cup matches in 2008, becoming an instant hero among fans!

BEST FOOT FORWARD!

Some players are more superstitious than others – Cristiano Ronaldo will always step onto the pitch right foot first!